A Father's Journey and a Son's Dream

By Dr Mohammed Fahim PhD

© 2017 Dr Mohammed Fahim PhD.
All rights reserved.

No part of this book may be reproduced in any written, electronic, recording, or photocopying form without written permission of the author, Dr Mohammed Fahim PhD, who may be contacted by emailing drmohammed.fahim@gmail.com.

BRAND AGENCY

Published by brandagency.com
ISBN: 9781520483849
First Edition

Dedication

This book and any proceeds from it are fully dedicated to my mosque (Qur'ani Murkuz Trust - South Woodford Muslim Community Centre) in South Woodford, London, England. I have been the Trust's Chairman and Head Imam of the mosque since they were established in 1994. This is a voluntary job and I do not receive any remuneration or financial gain from it. This mosque is known to be a centre of education and for delivering the true moderate and tolerant message of Islam. It empowers women and promotes integration in the West, without losing our faith or diluting our religion. It encourages multi-faith dialogue and respects British values, which in fact, are the same like Islamic values.

Contents

Acknowledgements

Introduction

Chapter 1

    The Fulfilment of Dreams: Joseph the Son of Jacob

    The Scene is Set

    Act I: Divine Visions

    Act II: The Well

    Act III: The Palace

    Act IV: The Prison

    Act V: The Famine

    Act VI: The Fulfilment of the Dream

    Act VII: The End?

Chapter 2

    The Sanctity of Divine Revelations

    2:1 Introduction

    2:2 What do Muslims Believe in?

    2:3 Islam was the Religion of Abraham

    2:4 Joseph in the Quran and the Old Testament

    2:4:1 'Introduction to Joseph (Yusuf)', Chapter 12, the Quran', by Abdullah Yusuf Ali

    2:4:2 'Joseph in the Qur'an' by John Kaltner

    2:5 The Torah and the Gospel in the Quran

Chapter 3

    Joseph in Art and Drama

    3:1 Introduction

3:2 Archaeological Evidence of Joseph in Egypt

3:3 Joseph in Art, 13th-19th Centuries

3:4 Joseph in Literature and Culture, 17th-18th Centuries

3:4:1 The Emergence of Joseph in Writing

3:4:2 Joseph in Teaching

3:4:3 Joseph in Literature

3:4:4 Joseph in Critical Thinking

3:4:5 Joseph: A Model of Virtue

3:5 Joseph in Film and Theatre

3:5:1 Joseph and the Amazing Technicolor Dreamcoat (Stage Production)

3:5:2 Sold Into Egypt (Original Title: Giuseppe venduto dai fratelli- Joseph and His Brethren) 1961 Yugoslavian/Italian Film

3:5:3 Joseph in Egypt (1995 TV Film)

3:5:4 Joseph King of Dreams (2000 Animated Film)

3:5:5 Prophet Joseph (Yusuf the Honest/ Yousuf e Payambar) 2008 Iranian TV Series

Bibliography

Acknowledgements

At the very outset, I would like to express my most sincere thanks to Abdullah Yusuf (Joseph) Ali for his great superlative work, "The Holy Quran: Text, Translation and Commentary".

I have been studying his work since 1970. It is, by far, the best known, most studied and most respected English translation of the Quran. The authenticity of Yusuf Ali's extensive scholarly commentaries and explanatory notes and its distinguishing characteristics have been a great source of inspiration, not only to me, but also to many others. I have referred to many of his comments whilst writing this book. May God reward him abundantly, forgive all his sins and admit him to His Gardens of Bliss.

Special thanks go to my researcher, Miss Basmah (Wafiqa) Busawon, for the research she carried out to establish the influence of the story of Joseph on art and drama throughout history. Also her input regarding editing the text and her artistic talents in organising the various chapters of the book were highly appreciated. She was a great inspiration to me.

A huge amount of credit is owed to my illustrator, Ms Irene F.M. Luitsz, for the magnificent artwork she provided to add life to the book. Her illustrations reflect her ingenuity in understanding the spirit of the story of Joseph and illuminate it in beautiful colours.

When it came to publishing the book, we had to explore different avenues. We concluded that the best way forward was to publish it as an eBook. >>

So God, in His Grace and Wisdom, put in my way Mr Yousuf (Joseph) Aslam of Amazing Publishing. He made my dream come true as he is the one who took upon his shoulders the full responsibility of publishing my first book. So many thanks to him.

It is amazing that two Josephs, Joseph Aly and Joseph Aslam, helped me in realising this book about "Joseph - the son of Jacob"!

Credit must also go to Mrs Mary Hossain and my daughter Dr Donia Fahim for their tremendous efforts in editing the text many years ago.

Introduction

I Have a Dream:

This book is about my dream of how to keep a family together.

It might be a good read for parents who are struggling to keep peace and tranquillity at home. It might also be a great help for members of the same family who have stopped talking to each other and have forgotten how to sing "we are family!"
It is very easy in life to despair, to lose patience and to run away from our responsibilities.

There was one Messenger of God who resigned his job. He physically ran away from his duties. He sent a message to God saying, "Dear God. I can't work for you anymore. You sent me to awful people who refuse to listen to me when I tell them about You. They ridiculed me, abused me and belittled me. They did not want to listen to Your Message. They preferred to worship an idol instead of You. I could not change their mind. I left them to You to deal with them."

O my God! How could he do that? He lost his job because he was so impatient. Did he consider the consequences before running away from his current Employer? Unfortunately, there are people in life who would just walk away from their employment or their marriage following an argument or a disagreement, leading to their families suffering because of bad planning and impatience.

So who was this Messenger of God who resigned his job and how did God deal with his resignation?

The Messenger was Jonah. His punishment was for a whale to swallow him up. He remained in the tummy of the whale for three days and three nights. Can you imagine the bad smell he had to tolerate, the darkness of the environment he lived in, the acid which was burning his skin, the pressure of the water on top of him and the psychological and spiritual pain he was going through for disappointing his Creator?

But what was he doing while he was in the tummy of the whale? Surely he was constantly regretting the decision he made in haste to resign his job and run away. He was saying all the time "I'm sorry. I was indeed wrong."

The Quran tells us in 21:87-88: "And remember Zun-nun (the man of the whale), when he departed in wrath. He imagined that We have no power over him. But he cried through the depth of darkness, 'There is no God but You. I was indeed wrong.' So We listened to him and delivered him from distress, and thus We do deliver those who have faith."

Then God forgave him and reinstated him and sent him back to the same people again. But this time Jonah learned his lesson. He persevered patiently to deliver God's Message to his people. He tolerated their insults and succeeded in persuading them to believe in the One True God.

Prophets are father-figures to their nations. Just like Jonah, we sever ties with our children, or our parents, when we cannot understand each other. We are quick to break the relationship when our ego has been bruised from insults or bad treatment. But from the story of Jonah, we also learn that relationships require effort. It takes hard work to maintain the ties of kinship and though it may be a difficult task, we cannot give up.

There are parents and children who are irresponsible, selfish, impatient and not willing to compromise. No one can deny that it is incredibly difficult to bring up children in today's world. As such, every father has many journeys to travel to fulfil the dreams of each one of his children. Each journey is bumpy, long and full of surprises. Many hurdles must be tackled and tidal waves to be surfaced.

For such a journey the father must equip himself with love and fear of God, patience, wisdom and courage. He should always seek God's help and guidance at all times to keep him on His Straight Path; that the journey will be short, safe, fast and successful with a happy ending. God's light would illuminate the unseen dark paths he has to travel.

His travel document will be God's Divine Revelations and his provisions for the journey will be fear of God. This will make him aware of his relationship with God and his relationship with others. "If provisions are required for a journey on earth, how much more important to provide for the final journey into the future world? The best of such provisions is right conduct, which is the same as the fear of God."[1]

And his dress code will be righteousness. "The body is pure and beautiful, as long as it is not defiled by misuse; its clothing and ornaments, good or bad, honest or meritorious, according to the inner motives which gave them colour...If good, they are the symbols of purity and beauty; but the best clothing and ornament we could have comes from righteousness, which covers the nakedness of sin, and adorns us with virtues."[2]

He as a father should build his foundation in this life on piety to God and seeking His Pleasure. "A man who builds his life on Piety (which includes sincerity and the purity of all motives) and his hopes on the Good

---

[1] Abdullah Yusuf Ali, 1990. *Holy Qur-ān: English Translation of "The Meanings and Commentary"*. p81.
[2] Yusuf Ali, 1990, p351.

Pleasure of God, builds on a firm foundation of rock that will never be shaken."[3]

In doing so, not only will the father have the strength to deal with the challenges he faces, but he will also provide a beautiful example of steadfastness to his children. In turn, we as parents must examine the ways in which God's Messengers dealt with their children's needs and aspirations and how did they help them to fulfil their dreams? They are our role models whom we must emulate.

Can my Children be my Enemies?

Whilst a father might be struggling to ensure the prosperity of his children, some members of his family might turn against him and become his enemies. How should we deal with this situation if it arises to save our family?

God tells us in 8:28 of the Quran that our possessions and our progeny are but a trial. "A big family-many sons-was considered a source of power and strength. So in English, a man with many children is said to have his 'quiver full;' Cf.Psalms, cxxvii. 4-5: 'As arrows are in the hands of a mighty man, so are the children of thy youth. Happy is the man that hath his quiver full of them; they shall not be ashamed, but they shall speak with the enemies in the gate.' So with property and possessions: they add to a man's dignity, power, and influence. But both possessions and a large family are a temptation and a trial. They may turn out to be a source of spiritual downfall, if

---

[3] Yusuf Ali, 1990, p469.

they are mishandled, or if the love of them excludes the love of God."[4]

And in the Quran, 64:14-15, God says: "O who you believe: Truly among your spouses and your children are (some that are) enemies to yourselves. So beware of them. But if you forgive and overlook, and cover up (their faults), surely God is Oft-Forgiving, Most Merciful. Your riches and your children may be but a trial, whereas God, with Him is the Highest Reward."

The above verses do refer to a specific incident where a wife acted in an irresponsible manner, however a husband may act in the same way and become an enemy to his wife.

"In some cases the demands of families, i.e., wife and children, may conflict with a man's moral and spiritual convictions and duties. In such cases he must guard against the abandonment of his convictions, duties, and ideals to their requests or desires. But he must not treat them harshly. He must make reasonable provision for them, and if they persist in opposing his clear duties and convictions, he must forgive them and not expose them to shame or ridicule, while at the same time holding on to his clear duty."[5]

Family Crises: Quality Time not Quality Gifts!

Are parents aware of the rights of their children? Did we choose a good father or a good mother for them?

---

[4] Yusuf Ali, 1990, p420.
[5] Yusuf Ali, 1990. p1479.

Did we give them good names? Do we treat boys and girls equally? Do we invest in their education? Do we spend time with them to impart Islamic manners and spiritual teachings, without making them radicals or extremists? Do we act as a good role model for them?

Do we encourage the boys to be pure and chaste until they get married? The role model for our boys is Joseph the son of Jacob who resisted the temptation of the most beautiful and influential women in Egypt, preferring to go to prison rather than doing something wrong.

Do we encourage our daughters to be pure and chaste until they get married? The role model for our girls is Mary the mother of Jesus who protected her chastity at a time when virginity was not that important and God gave her a child without a father.

We as parents must make an effort to spend quality time with our children to teach them Islamic values, which excel any manmade values. Most parents are very busy in their lives. They compensate their failure in spending time with their children by giving them quality gifts instead. If we do this, we have not fulfilled the rights of our children who deserve love, affection and knowledge of moral and spiritual teachings. It is important to invest in the proper upbringing of our children; not just financially but in terms of fostering healthy and open relationships between a parent and their child. In doing so, a child would be more committed to maintaining relationships with their parents in their old age.

We as parents must give thanks to God for giving us children. They are a gift from God. In the same way as we rejoice when we have a boy we must also rejoice when we have a girl. We should treat them equally. We can't give absolute freedom to the boys and favour them over the girls, or deny the girls the right to be educated or the right to choose their own husbands. There are no forced marriages in Islam and there is no honour killing in Islam. Treating our children with gentleness, love and respect is the greatest gift a parent can give.

Luqman the Wise Father

Luqman, as a sensible father, realised the importance of spending quality time with his son, to the extent that God praised him for this characteristic and honoured him in the Quran in Chapter 31. He was a very simple person, a carpenter by trade. In his wisdom, he prioritised his relationship with his son by sitting with him and spending quality time with him. The Quran does not tell us what questions the son asked, so the advice given by the wise father can be used without any limitations.

Let us examine what Luqman said to his son that caused him to be honoured by God. Luqman started every instruction by saying "O my son," which in Arabic is a loving address, full of kindness and warmth. Luqman was not harsh when instructing his son; he did not shout at him, or use threats and violence when teaching his son an important lesson. Rather, Luqman was gentle in his approach, using his son's curiosity as an opportunity to impart wisdom.

In the following verses, while Luqman was talking to his son, God incorporated instructions regarding how we should be kind to our parents. This is to emphasise the importance of honouring our parents even if they do not share the same beliefs as us. According to the Quran, 31: 12-16, "We bestowed wisdom on Luqman: 'Show your gratitude to God.' Any who is grateful does so to the profit of his own soul. But if any is ungrateful, verily God is free of all wants, worthy of all praise.' Luqman said to his son by way of instruction: 'O my son! Don't join in worship (others) with God, for false worship is indeed the highest wrong doing.'

And We have enjoined on man (to be good) to his parents. In travail upon travail did his mother bear him, and in two years was his weaning. (Hear the command), 'Show gratitude to Me and to your parents, to Me is your final goal. But if they strive to make you join in worship with Me things of which you have no knowledge, don't obey them. However, keep their company in this life with justice and consideration, and follow the way of those who turn to Me (in love). In the end the return of you all is to Me, and I will tell you all that you did.'

'O my son!' (Said Luqman), 'if there be but the weight of a mustard seed and it was hidden in a rock, or anywhere in the heavens or on earth, God will bring it out, for God understands the finest mysteries, and is well-acquainted with them.'

Luqman must have spent a lot of time explaining to his son the difference between right and wrong, taking pleasure in making the religion simple and accessible for his child. We can follow his example by taking every opportunity to impart small nuggets of wisdom to our children. For an example, Luqman explained to his son in the above verses that nothing is hidden from Allah's knowledge; is this not a lesson we could pass onto our children during a game of hide-and-seek?

The verses of this chapter continue (31:17-19), 'O my son! Establish regular prayers, enjoin what is just, and forbid what is wrong. And persevere patiently whatever (tests) may befall you, for this is firmness of purpose in the conduct of affairs. And don't swell your cheek (for pride) at people, nor walk in insolence through the earth, for God does not love any arrogant boaster. And be moderate in your pace, and lower your voice, for the harshest of all sounds without doubt is the braying of ass.

It is in Luqman's advice to be moderate in all aspects of life that we see this father's sincere concern for his child. Luqman's wisdom was in his ability to offer simple, comprehensive advice that applies to any given situation. In this way, we also see Luqman instil in his son the need to be mindful of God in every action, every day.

"The beginning of all wisdom is conformity with the Will of God. That means that we must understand our relations to Him and worship Him aright. Then we must be good to mankind, beginning with our own parents. For the two duties are not diverse, but one. Where they appear to conflict, there is something wrong with the human will."[6]

So Luqman wanted his son to have the best conduct in this life to guarantee his salvation in the hereafter. He was aware that on the Day of Judgement neither a son nor a father can benefit each other or be a substitute for each other. Each individual is

---

[6] Yusuf Ali, 1990. p1036.

responsible for his conduct. God confirms this in the same Chapter (31: 33), 'O man kind! do your duty to your Lord and fear (the coming of) a Day when no father can help his son, nor a son can help his father. Surely, the promise of God is true. Let not then this present life deceive you, nor let the Chief Deceiver (Satan) deceive you about God.' However in this life, a parent has a duty to benefit his child while he still can, by offering sincere advice on matters of conduct and acting as a role model.

The Purpose of Our Creation & Family Issues

Although I have been married for almost half a century, my wife and I are still having many unresolved issues. God says in 49:13 that He has created us all from a single pair of a male and female and made us into nations and tribes to get to know each other. So the purpose of creation is to create familiarity, not to ignore, despise or exploit each other.

If we all get to know each other we would have peace in our planet.

Do I really know my wife? Does she really know me?

I do not think so. If every husband and wife would make an effort to understand each other, many family issues would have been avoided.

Why do we argue with each other? Is it our ego which is running the show?

Why do we not say sorry when we do something wrong?

Why do we not appreciate each other and say thank you? Why do we look at faults in each other instead of looking for positive aspects and blow them up to cover our shortfalls?

I find Adam and Eve to be the best role model for a husband and wife. When they fell into temptation and ate from the forbidden tree, their honeymoon was over. They were kicked out of the Garden. But they both said sorry to God. They admitted their failure and God forgave them. They lost everything. But they never lost the love they had for each other and their faith in God's Forgiveness and Mercy. They never blamed each other or insulted each other. They did not walk away from each other. On the contrary they stayed together. If they would have left each other on that day, none of us would have been here today.

Then they went through another major test when one of their sons killed his brother out of jealousy. In spite of all the tests and the problems they had to go through, they never stopped communicating with each other.

Unfortunately, there are many family members who stop talking to each other, even with the availability of the most modern and sophisticated means of communication.

Some parents kick their children, not just out of the house, but completely shun them out of their lives. Why? Because the child may have committed something beneath the religious or cultural approval of their parents? Very sad!

Instead of trying to teach, guide, advise, tolerate, forgive, forget, overlook and embrace, they decide to write their children off and sever all channels of communication with them.

On the other hand, some children walk out from the house by choice and never come back or even call. Also very bad!

What about husbands and wives, who have been married for many years, yet find themselves hating each other? Then they can no longer tolerate or accommodate each other, leading to messy fights in law courts and the spending of life savings on solicitors' fees. Some of them may use their innocent children as bargaining chips.

The Holy Quran and the Tradition of Prophet Mohammed, peace be upon him, are full of guidance on how to resolve family disputes and how to help a family in crisis to achieve peace within. If both parties are willing to resolve their differences, God will help them as stated in the Quran, 4:35.

There is no marriage without problems. And there is no family which does not experience crises. A family that prays together, stays together.

How to Save a Family?

This book is about a large family which was torn into pieces by jealousy and hatred. The father and one of his twelve sons managed to put a very confusing and complicated jigsaw together to restore the family fabric. In the story of Joseph, Chapter 12, of the Holy Quran, I admire the way in which both Jacob and his son Joseph dealt with the other ten jealous Children of Israel. The first chapter of this book narrates the full story of the journey which Jacob had to travel in order to fulfil the dream of his son Joseph, and to save the rest of the Children of Israel from the wrath of God.

Both Joseph and Jacob suffered for a long time from the evil planning and plotting practised by these ten men. And in spite of this, they both embarked on a rehabilitation programme to save the souls of the Children of Israel. However, the father and his son each had a different plan to follow. When the children claimed that their younger brother Joseph was devoured by the wolf and brought back Joseph's shirt stained with false blood to convince their father of their tale, Jacob did not shout at them or beat them up or disown them. Instead, he declared to them that he is going to persevere patiently. Not only this, but he will enjoy being patient without any complaint and he will seek God's help and support in maintaining his patience regarding the tale they made up.

We all know that the majority of us, including myself, would really find it extremely difficult to enjoy being patient if we are hit with a calamity. Honestly, ask yourselves how would you have reacted if you were in Jacob's shoes? Personally, I would have beaten them all up and kicked them out of the house and deprived them from any inheritance!

O my God! This sounds very bad!

I only wanted to make a point to show how great Jacob was.

Jacob had two alternatives; either to kick his children out and write them off completely from his life, as the majority of us would have done or to try to save them from God's fury. Thank God Jacob in his wisdom chose the latter.

So how many parents today are willing to follow the example of Jacob? I promise I will change my approach and strive to follow his example!

He was the true role model of a loving, caring and compassionate father.

Was that the only thing he did?

No. He continued to communicate regularly with his children. He never stopped advising them whenever the need arose. He was so gentle and kind in the way he admonished them. As Jacob kept all communication channels open, it was easy for the ten sons to convince him to allow Benjamin to accompany them to Egypt, as requested by Joseph.

After the children pledged that they will take full care of Benjamin, the father's love was manifested again. He told them to be careful when they re-enter Egypt and they should enter it through different gates. He made it clear to them that he cannot protect them from whatever God has willed. Simply he meant to say, "I still love you and I wish you to be safe and sound, but I can't protect you from God's wrath."

When Jacob lost his sight because of his grief, he commanded his children to go back to Egypt to look for Joseph and Benjamin. He told them that they should never despair from the Soothing Mercy of God.

When the children returned to Egypt with Joseph's shirt and placed it on Jacob's face, he instantly regained his sight. The sons admitted their guilt and asked their father to ask for forgiveness for them. In fact they said, "Sorry! We were wrong doers."

The father immediately promised to ask for forgiveness for them from his Lord, the Oft-Forgiving, the Most Merciful.

How many parents are willing to forgive their children in spite of the pain, insult and hurt these children might have caused them? Was suffering not one of the conditions of a parent's journey to fulfil their child's dream?

Let us now examine Joseph's plan to save his ten brothers from God's wrath. Joseph embarked on a completely different rehabilitation programme. He was aware that his brothers were so jealous of him and Benjamin. They were liars, envious, crude, brute, evil and arrogant. An evil soul like this must be humiliated to get rid of the evils harboured there. For God to forgive them they must admit their guilt, say "Sorry," turn to God in repentance and ask for His forgiveness and the forgiveness of those whom they did hurt.

When the ten brothers came to Egypt the first time, Joseph welcomed them, showered them with affection and treated them generously, all the while keeping his true identity a secret. Joseph asked them to bring their brother Benjamin next time they come, otherwise there would be no more provisions for them. In the meantime he commanded his helpers to conceal in his brothers' saddles the goods they bartered with, so that they would soon return with Benjamin as they now have enough goods to trade once again.

The trick worked and as expected, they soon came back to Egypt for the second time, this time with their brother Benjamin in tow.

Joseph had another plan to detain his younger brother Benjamin. He ordered his helpers to conceal the King's cup in Benjamin's saddlebag. Then, just before the brothers' caravan was about to leave, a caller stopped them and accused them of theft. Each saddlebag was meticulously and personally searched by Joseph, until the cup was at last discovered in Benjamin's bag. The brothers instead of defending Benjamin, stated that, "He is a thief like his other brother (i.e. Joseph)."

Joseph concealed the insult and did not seek revenge, as he had to exercise patience if his plan was to succeed.

When the brothers once again returned to Egypt for the third time, they admitted their poverty before Joseph and their desperate need for grain. They begged Joseph to be charitable to them, especially now that they had no quality goods to barter with. Joseph felt that this was the right moment to disclose himself to them. Once he had revealed his true identity, Joseph even found an excuse for them regarding the evil ways in which they treated him and his brother. He simply said to them, "Surely you were not aware of what you did, you did not mean it, and you were ignorant when you did that!"

Joseph claimed that it was Satan to be blamed for sowing enmity between him and his brothers. Should we then blame Satan for our sins? Of course not. Satan says, as mentioned in the Quran, 14:22; "Don't blame me, blame yourselves. I simply called you and you came running after me!"

So if we resist the temptations of the Evil One, we will please our Maker and achieve salvation. But whenever we fall into temptation because of our weakness, we must repent and ask for forgiveness and make an effort not to do it again. Our salvation is in sincere repentance.

When the brothers recognised Joseph, they immediately admitted their guilt and that God had favoured and honoured Joseph above all of them; they asked for forgiveness and admitted their fault. Joseph immediately forgave them without any reproach. He told them that God would forgive them;

Joseph's plan, as inspired by God, was fulfilled and he saved the souls of his brothers from God's disgrace and terrible punishment. Honestly, ask yourselves how many brothers or sisters are willing to swiftly forgive each other without reproach?

To benefit from the beautiful examples of the prophets, you have to be a very caring and patient parent who has full faith in God, or a very obedient child who strives to resist Satan's temptations and fears God at all times.

I'm a Believer

Whenever I talk about Biblical prophets such as Abraham, Ishmael, Isaac, Jacob, Joseph, Jonah, Moses and Jesus, people ask me: Aren't you a Muslim? Aren't you a follower of Mohammed? Why are you talking about prophets from the Old Testament? Are these prophets mentioned in the Quran too? Therefore, I have briefly explained in Chapter 2 of this book what Muslims believe in.

I have also illustrated in this chapter how Islam is in fact an Abrahamic faith. In doing so, I will demonstrate how the Torah (the Old Testament), the Gospel (the New Testament) and the Quran are revered and respected in Islam, as believing in them is one of the articles of faith in Islam.

How Did the Story of Jacob and Joseph Influence Art and Drama?

From ancient Egypt to the present day, Joseph has been a figure through which people have recognised their religious, moral and political ideals. The proliferation of paintings, etchings, literature, plays, sermons and literary criticisms that emerged over the 16th and 17th centuries is proof of Joseph's strong presence in Europe's social consciousness. Through these various mediums, Joseph was extolled as a model of piety, endurance, forgiveness and chastity.

The story of Joseph, as expressed in art and drama, had the dual purpose of entertaining and educating; the story was a definitive moral tale passed down from parents to children in 17th century Europe, and continued to serve as an example later in life for adults too. Joseph's tale was often dramatised and preached in large social gatherings to encourage adults to live godly, virtuous lives in the face of social unrest. Therefore by the 17th century, Joseph was viewed as a potent religious icon, whose example was central to forming decent familial and social relationships.

This being said, Joseph fell from the European public consciousness over the 18th century, as the French Revolution redefined ideas of the relevancy of Biblical figures in political and social life. This book, however, will trace Joseph's substantial cultural impact over the 20th and 21st centuries. Through film, television and animation, Joseph has emerged as an honourable figure for families today; we learn through his example that we all have unique gifts that can help us overcome any obstacle, and that we all have the capacity to forgive.

Chapter 1

The Fulfilment of Dreams: Joseph the Son of Jacob

The Scene is Set

This adventure is one of the greatest in history. It begins in a small town in the Holy Land of Canaan, where a struggle between the forces of good and evil was about to take place.

At the first light of dawn, the town could be seen from the surrounding hilltops. It was a bustling place, for the economy was based on trade. All kinds of goods could be found there, each for sale in a different area of the town; spice sellers in one place with huge mounds of brightly-coloured powders spreading a delicious aroma in the air; cloth sellers with bales of fabric from distant lands; fruit sellers with beautifully arranged displays of ripe produce. Large caravans of camels on their way to Egypt often passed this way, returning to their homeland laden with merchandise from all neighbouring countries. It was in this prosperous and sociable little town that a young boy called Joseph lived. From the day he was born, he seemed bathed in peace and happiness, a sign of the spirit of God. He was one of the fortunate few chosen by God to undertake a mission. He was no ordinary child.

One beautiful, fresh morning, Joseph woke to hear the birds singing their rich songs of praise to God. Among the birds greeting the newborn day were two snow-white rock doves, their shining bodies appearing translucent against the bright sun. Joseph lay watching them and thinking about a strange and beautiful vision he had experienced during the night. As soon as he woke up, he knew that the dream was important...

Act I: Divine Visions

In his dream, Joseph was dressed in fine clothes. He had watched in amazement as the sun, the moon and eleven stars bowed down before him. It was all very strange. When he awoke, he ran to tell his father Jacob, who gazed tenderly at him and said, 'What a glorious dream, my beloved son. May God always bless you.'

Upon hearing his son's dream, Jacob began to reflect on his grandfather, Abraham. In spite of Abraham's old age, he never let his family down or ignored any of his responsibilities. He remembered that his uncle Ishmael was born when Abraham was 86 years old (Genesis 16:16) and his father Isaac was born when Abraham was 100 years old (Genesis 21:5) from a barren and aged Sarah. Upon reflecting on the miraculous birth of his father Isaac, Jacob also remembered how Sarah was informed of the birth of her future grandson, Jacob himself, by the angels. With this, Jacob knew that divine visitations had come to his ancestors before and that what Joseph had experienced was no ordinary dream.

Jacob's mind reached back in time as he recalled the great sacrifices offered by his elderly grandfather Abraham and his uncle Ishmael, in response to a vision received by Abraham when Ishmael was still just a child. When Ishmael reached the age of consent, Abraham saw in a dream that God had commanded him to offer Ishmael, his only son at the time, in sacrifice. When Abraham informed his son of this, Ishmael said without any hesitation, 'O my father! Do as you are commanded. You will find me so patient by God's will.' Even Abraham's wife Hagar did not object to God's command. She fully submitted her will to God's will.

As Abraham laid Ishmael prostrate, his forehead on the ground in preparation for the sacrifice, God called out to him.

'O Abraham! You have already fulfilled the dream. Thus indeed We reward those who do right. That surely was a great trial!'

And God ransomed Ishmael with a momentous sacrifice by commanding Abraham to slaughter a ram instead of his son.

When Jacob reflected on the vision of his grandfather and the birth of his father, he knew that no matter how terrible or impossible these visions may be, God will always facilitate a beautiful outcome. As such, Jacob had full faith that, even though Joseph's vision seemed strange, God would fulfil it for the good of all. But Jacob also anticipated great difficulty; he knew that he would be tested like his ancestors and that he would have to face these tests with patience and righteousness.

Jacob loved his two youngest boys, Joseph and Benjamin, very much and gave them more attention than he did to the others, especially when the death of Rachel left them without a mother to look after them. The other ten brothers, knowing their father's great love for Joseph and Benjamin, had become very jealous.

Jacob was a wise, religious man who could see that Joseph, even as a child, was full of the Spirit of God. He foresaw that among all his sons, it was Joseph who would be chosen by God for a very special destiny. The ten stepbrothers had been led astray by Satan, the evil force that had put unkind and selfish thoughts into their minds. Their jealousy might make them plot against Joseph and harm him. So when Joseph told Jacob about the dream, his father became afraid for him and begged his son not to mention the dream to his brothers.

Jacob warned Joseph about his danger and said to him, 'My dear little son, don't relate your vision to your brothers, lest they plot evil against you. Satan is the sworn enemy of man. You may not understand the meaning of your vision now, but God will choose you and teach you to interpret visions. He is All-Wise and All-Knowing. Have faith in Him, as your forefathers Isaac and Abraham did.'

Act II: The Well

The ten older brothers envied and hated Joseph and Benjamin. Jacob had the wisdom to see that his two, young and innocent sons needed protection and that Joseph in particular had spiritual greatness within him. But to his ten other sons, Jacob's wisdom was only folly or madness because it opposed their own sense of self-love, as the truth often does. Thus they relied on the brute strength of numbers-the ten hefty brethren against Jacob, Joseph, and Benjamin- in order to carry out their evil plot.

The ten brothers were watching from a distance with jealousy and hatred in their eyes when they saw Joseph and Benjamin sitting on their father's knee.

'We are just as good as those two; our father is an old fool!' whispered one of the brothers. 'We are always being told, 'Why can't you be good like Joseph!' He is always talking about Joseph. He has no consideration at all for our hard work.'

'Something will have to be done,' another brother said. 'We will have to get rid of Joseph. Kill him or cast him out to some unknown land. There will be plenty of time to turn over a new leaf later. Once Joseph is out of the way, we can make a good impression on our father and he will love and favour us as much as he loves and favours Joseph now.'

'Don't kill Joseph,' said the older brother, who was perhaps a little kinder than the others, or perhaps he simply did not want to be accused of murder. 'Let us leave him at the bottom of a well north of here. Then we will not be guilty of his blood on our hands and maybe some travellers passing by will find him and take him to a far country. Whatever happens, at least we will be rid of him without actually killing him.'

The others agreed. 'At least this way we will not be responsible for his death. And later we can pretend to be good like him, or to repent of our crime after we have had all its benefits.' Sadly, Satan made their sinful acts seem alluring to them.

They went to see their father.

'Father, will you allow Joseph to come with us tomorrow? He can enjoy himself and play, and we shall take every care of him.'

They saw Jacob's reluctance. He did not know what was in their minds, but he had strong suspicions.

'I shall miss him if you take him with you, and I shall worry about him. Suppose a wolf comes and drags him away while you are busy and not looking after him?' Jacob said.

'Don't you trust us?' replied the eldest. 'There are ten of us. Surely the wolf would have to get past us before it could get near Joseph.'

Then Joseph pleaded with his father, 'Please, I should like to go.'

Although he loved his father dearly, he was also anxious to prove that he too could go on a journey like his brothers. Jacob hesitated and then agreed, persuaded by the brothers' arguments and by Joseph's plea.

It was hot the next day when the party set off, with Joseph running ahead. After some hours they reached the well and stopped to rest. After they had eaten they played games and ran races. Joseph was beginning to tire and the oldest brother said, 'Come and sit by me and have a rest.' While Joseph slept the brothers schemed and, in low voices, discussed what to do. They devised a cunning plan. The eldest son shook Joseph awake.

Update your details in just a few easy steps

 Get the answers to all your questions

Win luxury prizes in our monthly prize draw

 Get motoring advice and member offers

rac.co.uk

*We've given you this saving against the average quote for this level of cover from August to October 2016. Prices shown in your payment schedule include this saving. ΔUp to 20 miles from the garage, payment needs to be made upfront and the RAC will reimburse you, terms & conditions apply. ¹Payment method and frequency must match that chosen for your breakdown cover. European Rescue is only available as an annual payment. †The RAC Shop offer excludes car batteries. One transaction only. Please quote your discount code CRRra7365. Offer cannot be used in conjunction with any other offer.

Lines open Weekdays 8am - 8pm, Weekends 9am - 5pm, Bank Holidays 9am - 5pm. 03 numbers are charged at national call rates and included in inclusive minute plans from landlines and mobiles. Calls may be monitored and/or recorded.

Breakdown cover arranged and administered by RAC Financial Services Ltd (Registered No 05171817) and provided by RAC Motoring Services (Registered No 01424399) and/or RAC Insurance Ltd (Registered No 02355834). Registered in England; Registered Offices: RAC House, Brockhurst Crescent, Walsall WS5 4AW. RAC Motoring Services and RAC Financial Services Ltd are authorised and regulated by the Financial Conduct Authority in respect of insurance mediation activities. RAC Insurance Ltd is authorised by the Prudential Regulation Authority and regulated by the Financial Conduct Authority and the Prudential Regulation Authority.

Alex Heath
Head of Membership

'Joseph, wake up! I've lost the ring father gave me. It dropped into the well. If we lowered you in the bucket, could you try and find it for us?'

Joseph was by far the lightest and smallest and the obvious one to choose for this difficult task, so without any suspicion of their real motives, he gladly did what his brothers asked. Yet when the bucket reached the bottom, the brothers cut the rope. At first, Joseph thought that the rope had broken and somehow his brothers would rescue him, even as their voices faded away. There was little light and the walls were wet and cold. For a while Joseph believed his brothers would return, but as the hours passed he realised that they had left him to die. The only comfort left to him was his faith in the love and mercy of God. His spirit remained strong and his courage did not fail him. Indeed it was now, when the situation seemed hopeless, that God comforted him by putting into his heart the idea that, some day, his brothers would need him; that one day Joseph would be in a position to help them and that he would do so gladly, making them ashamed of the way they were treating him now.

The brothers returned home in the early part of the night, ready with a tale they had invented to explain to their father why Joseph had not come back with them. It was dark and Jacob dimly saw the faces of his ten sons as he looked anxiously for Joseph. They pretended to weep as they spoke.

'Father, we were having a race and we left Joseph to look after our things. When we returned, a wolf had dragged him away and devoured him. We know you don't believe us, even though we are telling the truth.'

Jacob staggered, as if from a blow. He shook his head in disbelief.

'O my beloved son, my dear one!'

As proof, the eldest brother held up the coat Joseph had worn, the coat of beautiful colours that Jacob had given him, the coat they had stained red with an animal's blood.

'It is the truth,' they said.

Jacob held the coat to him and slowly sank to his knees. He looked up at them in despair.

'No, I cannot believe you. You have made up this tale. Your souls have tempted you to do something evil. Ah! What is there left for me now that my beloved son has gone?'

But even in his despair Jacob's faith was strong. 'I ask God for patience. Only God can help me to bear the loss you speak of.'

In fact, Jacob had two options: either to behave in a godly way or to condemn, disown and throw out his children, as many parents of today may have done. In choosing the former option, Jacob embarked on a long-term rehabilitation plan to bring his children back to God's Straight Path. Jacob knew that the best way to save his children from God's anger was to persevere patiently, have faith in God's soothing mercy and to always maintain communication with his children.

The following day, when the sun was in the middle of the sky, a caravan of travellers reached the well where Joseph was; naturally their first task was to draw water. Deep in the well, Joseph heard them talking as a bucket came down towards him. Although he was exhausted and weak from hunger, he managed to catch hold of the bucket. He clung tight to it and felt himself slowly being raised to the surface. Imagine the merchants' surprise when this heavy bucket produced not water, but a young and handsome boy.

'This is amazing! What good fortune,' they exclaimed. 'Here is a fine boy who does not belong to anyone and whom we can sell for a large sum of money in the slave market in Egypt. What a treasure!'

Suddenly there was a noise behind him. Two of Joseph's brothers had returned to the spot and had been watching to see what would happen to him.

'This boy belongs to us,' said one. 'He is a runaway slave. We were looking for him.'

What an evil statement made by this brother! Poor Joseph, how did he feel? It was his faith that prevented him from responding. Joseph now realised that home was a dangerous place; it was safer to be a slave than it was to be alone with his brothers. Despite the anguish this must have caused him, Joseph knew that all that God wills is for the best.

The travellers thought the older brother's story was unlikely, but asked anyway, 'What do you intend to do with him?'

The brothers hesitated and looked at one another. 'He's more trouble than he's worth; it's time we got rid of him,' they said.

They settled on a miserable price and so Joseph was sold into slavery for a handful of silver coins.

Now we can see how everyone in this story reacted differently according to their limited view of the situation. Joseph, in spite of his faith, must have felt hurt at his brothers' betrayal. Jacob, though patient, was sunk in grief at the loss of the son he loved so much. The brothers, delighted with the success of their plan, had managed to get rid of Joseph. Finally the merchants were congratulating themselves on acquiring a handsome youth at such a bargain. All of them only saw part of the picture. God, who knows everything, knew all their feelings, motives and deeds, was working out His own plan. None of us know where our destiny is leading us; we cannot see how, in God's plan, evil will eventually be defeated and good will overcome everything. None of us had any choice before coming to this life. We do not know when or how or where we are going to die. We cannot even push death away or ask for respite when it comes to us. So the wise person is the one who believes in the One True God, does not associate any partners with Him in any form, strives patiently and performs good deeds in this life to achieve salvation in the hereafter. That was the plan of Jacob and Joseph, both of whom put their full trust in God to defeat Satan the Evil One and save the Children of Israel who were destined to carry the torch of God into the Holy Land.

Act III: The Palace

So the caravan, taking Joseph as a slave, travelled on towards Egypt. The merchants were not mistaken; there were indeed many people ready to bid for this handsome, intelligent youth. There was great competition to buy him, but all were outbid by an honourable lord, a great Egyptian court dignitary. The lord was elderly and childless. When he saw Joseph, the idea came to him that he could buy Joseph as a slave and then perhaps later adopt him as his son. By having a son like Joseph, he would gain in dignity and esteem at the court. Therefore, the lord bought Joseph from the merchants and took him back to his palace, where he presented him to his wife Zulaikha.

'Make his stay among us good and honourable,' he told her, 'maybe he will bring us good fortune. Perhaps we shall adopt him as a son.'

This is the miracle of God's plan. From being sold into slavery at the well, Joseph was now established in a noble home in Egypt. God has full power over all things. However, most people do not know this.

Zulaikha was very young and loved her husband as a daughter loves a father. As she looked at Joseph, she was reminded of a man she had seen in a dream long ago, a dream she had kept secret and cherished in her heart. In her dream, she had been promised that this was the man she would marry.

Some years passed and Joseph grew from a youth to a young man. Although he grew up in the most luxurious surroundings at the Egyptian court, he also witnessed the corruption, the struggle for power and the immorality of life in the palace. Despite this, he kept his qualities of dignity and modesty and was honest and truthful in all that he did. God bestowed on him sound judgement and knowledge, as God will always reward those who do good deeds.

In this way, God established Joseph in Egypt, so that He might teach him to see the reality behind dreams and events. Through Joseph, the people of Egypt and the whole world would learn of the goodness and the wisdom of God.

But Zulaikha, remembering the young man of her dream and witnessing how Joseph grew in goodness and nobility, came to love him more and more. Gradually her love for him overwhelmed her. She found excuses for herself in her mind; *I am not really the lord's wife. He is my husband in name only. He is more like a father to me. I am sure that Joseph loves me. I must have him.* Surely these were immoral thoughts!

One evening, she ordered Joseph to come to her room. Her heart thudding, her body trembling, she shut the door behind him and locked it in haste. Turning to face him, she said, 'You know that I love you. Come my dear one. Take me. I'm all yours.'

Joseph stepped back startled. 'God forbid! Your husband is my master and has been so good to me, treating me like a son. I must be faithful to him and so must you. What you are asking me to do is wrong, and no good will ever come of it.'

His plea had no effect on her; she was completely overwhelmed by her passion for him. Indeed he too, as a human being with natural human emotions, would have given in to her, but he knew that it was wrong. She thought that no one could see behind closed doors, but he knew that God sees everything and his faith guided him. But there was no point in arguing with her.

'I must go,' he said, and made quickly for the door.

Zulaikha ran after him, tearing his shirt as she tried to pull him back.

Joseph managed to open the door and came suddenly to a halt. Outside the door were his master, the lord, and a young boy who was Zulaikha's cousin.

There was a shocked silence. Then Zulaikha cried, 'He tried to assault me. You must put him in prison or flog him. He must be punished severely for trying to seduce your wife.'

'It was she who tried to seduce me.' Joseph spoke with quiet dignity and truth, without anger or bitterness.

Then the young boy, who had been looking carefully at all that was happening, said with the clear-sightedness and frankness of a child, 'If his shirt is torn at the front, then her tale is true and he is a liar, but if his shirt is torn from the back, then he must be telling the truth and she is a liar.' Amazing judgement! That this child could think so logically in such a tense situation!

When the lord saw that the shirt was indeed torn from the back, he knew Joseph had spoken the truth. Now he had to decide what to do. As a high-ranking officer of state, he was in a very difficult position as such a scandal would likely undermine his high status in society. He was an old man, who had improved his own dignity and rank by marrying this noble and beautiful princess. She was young and impetuous, but he was sure that Joseph was innocent.

'I know you women and your tricks. Your evil planning is great indeed. Joseph, please do not tell anyone about this incident. My wife, ask for forgiveness for your sin for truly you have been at fault.'

Zulaikha was bitter and humiliated. *How can my husband possibly understand my feelings for Joseph?* She said to herself.

Joseph was true to his promise not to tell anyone about the incident, but Zulaikha was unable to keep silent. Rumours of the scene at the palace quickly began to spread through the city and soon the upper-class women began to gossip;

'The wife of the great lord has tried to seduce her slave.'

'She has such a passion for him.'

'She is clearly going astray.'

The rumours grew more and more exaggerated and distorted. When Zulaikha heard of this malicious talk she was very upset. How could the women of the city have any idea of the secret dream of her heart, or of the noble beauty of Joseph?

If only they could see how handsome Joseph is, they would not blame me, she thought. To justify herself in the eyes of these women, Zulaikha made a plan; first she would invite all the society ladies to a grand banquet.

In the banqueting hall the ladies reclined on silk cushions. They had drunk many glasses of wine and now they relaxed, at ease after such a splendid meal. They whispered and gossiped about their hostess and the rumours that were spreading about her love for her slave.

The dessert was being served and each of them had a knife to peel the fruit when Zulaikha suddenly announced, 'Ladies, I have a surprise for you!' The door was flung open and Joseph walked into their midst. Immediately there was a flutter of surprise and delight as all the ladies turned to look at him. So distracted were they by his beauty that they cut their hands without realising what they were doing.

'How beautiful he is!' they exclaimed, 'God preserve us; he can't be a man, he must be a noble angel!'

Zulaikha was triumphant.

'This is Joseph, the man you blame me for! Would you not have reacted in the same way as I did? See, you have lost control of yourselves to such an extent that you have cut your hands! I did try to seduce him, but he rejected me.'

She paused, furious with Joseph for rejecting her. Seeking the support of the other women, she continued. 'But now, if he does not do as I say, I shall have him thrown into prison. Let us see if he will change his mind when he has to exchange the luxury of the palace for a dark prison cell!'

Joseph called upon God, 'O my Lord! I would prefer prison to what these women are inviting me to do. And if You don't avert their guile from me, I may yield to them and so become one of the ignorant.' So his Lord answered him and warded off their evil planning, as He is All-Knowing and All-Hearing.

Joseph knew that as a human being he was weak and that without the help of God, he would not have been able to resist this new attack on his virtue. Zulaikha's ruse had revealed that she was not alone in her fascination of Joseph and her desire to seduce him. They all thought that the threat of prison would be enough to weaken Joseph, but God gave him the strength to prefer prison to a life of corruption at court.

The lord and all the noblemen of the court also thought that Joseph, although innocent, would have to be imprisoned if they were ever to restore order to their households. Joseph had caused such chaos among the women that the only solution seemed to be to remove him from society for a while.

How many young men today are willing to remain pure and chaste until they get married? It is no wonder that Joseph is the role model of purity and chastity among men. Similarly Mary, the mother of Jesus, is the role model of purity and chastity among women.

Act IV: The Prison

So it was that Joseph, although guilty of no crime, was sent to prison. The people at court all had their own reasons for putting him there. But beyond their limited view, God was putting into effect His universal plan. The injustice of the lord and the plotting of the women would nevertheless lead to goodness and mercy. The prison cell brought back unpleasant memories of the time Joseph had spent in the well: the cold and dank stone walls, the dim light. Joseph shivered, but he felt no bitterness at this new turn of events. He remembered how God was with him then; surely He was with him now.

Two men were sent to prison at about the same time as Joseph. Both were court officials who were in disgrace. One was the chief steward, whose duty was to prepare the King's wines and drinks; the other was a baker who prepared the King's bread. In prison, they both had vivid dreams which puzzled them. Seeing that Joseph was wise, that he was kind and honest and would use his wisdom to help even strangers, they asked him for the meanings of these dreams.

One, whose dream had given him a feeling of hope, said, 'In my dream I saw myself pressing grapes for wine.'

The other, whose dream filled him with apprehension, said, 'I was carrying bread on my head and the birds were eating from it.'

'Could you tell us the meaning of these dreams', they asked, 'We see that you are a wise man who does good to all.'

Joseph replied, 'God has given me the ability to help you and very soon, before we have our next meal, be sure I will tell you the meaning of your dreams; but first let me tell you about my belief in God. I have abandoned the ways of the people around me who do not believe in God and even deny that there is life after death. I follow the path of my forefathers – Abraham, Isaac and Jacob. God has taught us never to attribute partners to Him, just as He has taught all mankind. But people have turned away from this Truth and have invented many gods. I speak to you as one prisoner to another: How could anyone believe that many lords, all fighting among themselves, could be better than the One True God? The gods you name are nothing but your inventions, without any reality behind them. The only reality is God; authority can only come through Him. He has commanded us to worship Him alone and no other. If people reject Him, then it is they who will suffer through their own fault. Believe in the One God and you will be successful in this life and in the life after death. This is your only true hope.'

Only after he had explained to them these important truths, which would give them comfort and support whatever their fate might be, did Joseph answer their questions about their dreams.

'Fellow prisoners, the one who dreamt about pressing grapes for wine will once more pour out the wine for his master. The other, unfortunate man will hang from the cross and the birds of the air will eat from his head. The matter about which you have been seeking my opinion has been so decreed.'

Then he said to the one who would be released from prison, 'Mention me to the King when you return to the court.'

Joseph felt that he had spent long enough in prison; how could he carry out all that God wanted him to do while he was cast off in a cell? A few days later, as Joseph had foretold, the steward left the prison, but he was so overjoyed at regaining his freedom and the comfort of his old lifestyle that Satan made the steward forget the suffering of Joseph.

Then, one day, the King called the Council of his advisers together to relate to them a dream which he could not understand and which was preying on his mind.

'I saw a vision of seven fat cows being devoured by seven thin cows, and there were seven green ears of corn and seven withered ears. Is there anyone who can tell me the meaning of this dream?'

No one wanted to take the responsibility of interpreting the dream, so the councillors replied "We do not know how to interpret dreams, these are just nightmares."

But suddenly the steward's conscience was awakened. He remembered Joseph still in prison, and remembered how skilled he was in the interpretation of dreams. He also thought that he might get some credit himself for satisfying the King's request, so instead of mentioning Joseph immediately, he asked for time to go away and reflect upon the meaning of the dream.

Straightaway he went to the prison and spoke to Joseph.

'O Joseph!' he said, 'O man of truth! The King has had a dream and no one can tell him the meaning of it.' He then recounted how the seven lean cows had devoured the seven fat cows and how there were seven withered ears of corn and seven green ears.

To his surprise, Joseph did not reproach him for having forgotten him for so long in prison, but simply gave him the interpretation of the dream.

'For seven years you must cultivate the land diligently and from the harvest you should take a little for the people to eat and store the rest. After this there will be seven years of famine, during which time the stored grain can be used to feed the people; but you must keep a little for seed to sow when the famine is ended. After the drought will come a year in which there will be abundant water and you will press wine and oil once again.'

The steward hurried back to the King to give him this interpretation and to inform him of Joseph. Of course the King wanted to see Joseph for himself, and immediately sent a messenger to fetch him. The messenger expected Joseph to be overjoyed at this summons to appear at court, but first Joseph wanted to be sure that he was not returning to the same toxic environment that he had left behind.

'Go back to your lord and ask him of the ladies who cut their hands, and what their intention was. My Lord knows well their guile,' Joseph said to the King's messenger.

Joseph did not know if the King was aware of all the mischief that had gone on, and he needed to be free from the persecution of these ladies if he was to accomplish the task that God had destined for him. He was careful not to mention Zulaikha who, after all, had been kind to him and who was young and immature when she tried to attract him.

The messenger conveyed this message to the King, who sent for the ladies; Zulaikha also came with them.

'What was this affair about?' he asked. 'Tell me the whole truth.' Reluctantly the women admitted that Joseph had done nothing wrong.

Then Zulaikha spoke. 'I will tell you the whole truth. Joseph is completely innocent. It was I who tried to seduce him. I take the blame entirely on myself.'

During the long years when Joseph had been in prison, Zulaikha had suffered a great deal and her lust for him had changed into a true and selfless love. She had been inspired by the example of Joseph, calm and patient in every turn of fortune. Her husband, the old lord, was now dead; perhaps now, in spite of her sin, she could be worthy of Joseph.

She continued, 'I say this so that Joseph may know that I have never plotted against him or been false to him in his absence. I realise that God will never allow such evil plans to succeed. I do not say that I am blameless. Human beings are so easily inclined to evil unless God, through His mercy, helps them to be good. And surely God forgives and is All-Merciful.'

Now that Joseph's innocence, wisdom, truthfulness and trustworthiness had been proven and confirmed before all the court, the King sent for him.

'You have been treated most unfairly', he said. 'Because of your honesty and wisdom, I should like to appoint you to a high position in the court. What post can I offer you?'

'Thanks be to God that the truth has been revealed!' exclaimed Joseph. 'There are hard years ahead for the whole country. I should be honoured if you would put me in charge of the granaries and store houses of the land. I will look after them and see that there are enough supplies to last through the years of famine. I have knowledge and I'm trustworthy.'

These credentials of possessing knowledge and being trustworthy further established Joseph in the land. He was not interested in living a life of idle luxury; rather, he took on the most difficult task in order to help the people.

And so it was that this youth who had been left for dead at the bottom of a cold, dark well, who had been sold into slavery for a handful of coins by his jealous brothers, who had later been unjustly accused and imprisoned, was now a chief minister in the most magnificent empire of the day. In this way God provided an example for everyone, then and now, of goodness and faith; of purity and selflessness; of patience in adversity and trust in God. Joseph's faith had never faltered and his goodness was now rewarded, as God always rewards the efforts of those who persevere patiently and do good deeds. But Joseph knew that even better than the reward in this life is the reward with God in the life after death.

Act V: The Famine

Joseph, guided by God's wisdom and knowledge, directed the preparations for the predicted famine. The times of prosperity went by. The years of drought then came as foreseen, devastating both Egypt and its neighbouring countries alike. But Joseph had planned well and Egypt had enough corn to supply the people and even to sell to those who came from other starving lands. All were treated with courtesy and sold a carefully measured quota of grain.

With all this responsibility, Joseph never forgot his father and his brother, Benjamin. Would they have enough to eat in these difficult times? Would the other brothers persecute Benjamin as they had persecuted him? Then one day, driven by the famine in their own country, the ten brothers arrived in Egypt to buy corn and came face to face with their long-lost brother.

They did not recognize Joseph; all they saw was a high-ranking Egyptian official, dressed in the Egyptian way, surrounded by his servants and staff. But Joseph immediately recognized them and without revealing his identity, entered into conversation with them. How long had they been travelling? Where was their father and why had he not come with them? Had they left any other brothers at home with their old father?

Once he started them talking about Benjamin, Joseph said, 'You must bring him with you next time. I should like to see him.'

The brothers were very reluctant to agree to this, but Joseph was insistent. 'You see how well I am treating you here; bring your step brother next time, or I shall give orders that you receive no more corn from Egypt.'

If the brothers were puzzled by the concern of this great court official for their brother Benjamin, they did not show it. They were only too anxious to be given permission to return for more grain when their current supply was exhausted. So they said, 'We shall certainly ask our father if we can bring him next time, if that is what you wish.'

To encourage them to come again, Joseph ordered his servants to put back secretly into his brothers' saddlebags the goods they had brought with them to exchange for the corn. This way, they would be able to bring the same goods back with them to exchange for more food on their next journey.

When the brothers returned home they told Jacob all that had happened.

'We will not be given any more corn unless we return with our brother, Benjamin,' they said, 'so please send him with us so that we can buy more food. We will take good care of him.'

It was no easy task to persuade Jacob to let them take Benjamin; Jacob did not trust them at all after the loss of Joseph. 'Why should I trust you with him, when I trusted you with his brother before?' he said. 'But

God is the best to take care of him and He is the most Merciful.' Jacob knew that, whatever happened, only God could protect his son.

Then, when the brothers opened their baggage, imagine their surprise when they found that their goods had been returned to them. 'Look, father!' they exclaimed. 'Our goods have been sent back with us. Now we can take them again and get more food for our families. But we must take Benjamin with us. Do let him come! We shall take good care of him and return with an extra camel laden with provisions!'

At last Jacob replied, 'I will never send him with you unless you swear a solemn oath, in God's name, that you will bring him safely back to me unless you yourselves are prevented from returning.'

The brothers agreed and, when they had sworn their solemn oath, Jacob said, 'Over all that we say, May God be our Witness and our Guardian!'

Then, hoping to lessen the danger to his sons, he gave them some practical advice. 'My sons, when you enter the city, do not all go in by the same gate. Rather, all of you should enter from different gates. But no matter what advice I give you, only God can protect you. Above all put your trust in Him.'

So the brothers did as their kind and caring father said, but this human attempt to ward off danger did not in any way prevent God's plan from being carried out.

Now once more the brothers came into the presence of Joseph. He received them hospitably, even more so than he had done before and he asked the brothers if they had brought Benjamin with them. He then invited them to dine with him that evening and Joseph saw to it that Benjamin sat next to him. He made arrangements for them to stay in various houses, but invited Benjamin to stay in his own palatial quarters. Thus Joseph and Benjamin were able to spend some time alone together.

As soon as the other brothers had left, Joseph turned to Benjamin and said, 'I am your brother Joseph. Do not be upset at the way your brothers have been treating you.'

Benjamin stared in disbelief. Was this really his missing brother? This man was a government official at the court of Egypt. How did he come this far? Joseph explained everything and told him that he now had a plan and, whatever strange things happened, Benjamin was to keep silent.

The next day, when the brothers had collected their corn to take home, Joseph secretly hid the King's silver measuring cup in Benjamin's saddlebag. Then, just as they were slowly making their way out of the city there came a shout from one of the guards at the city gates.

'You in the caravan! Stop!'

The brothers, turning in astonishment, inquired, 'What's happened? Why are you stopping us?'

'The King's silver cup is missing. You must have stolen it. We have to check your baggage. There is a reward of a camel-load of corn for anyone who will find it and I'm in charge of this.' The guard's face was dark with anger.

The brothers protested, 'We did not come here to make trouble. We are not thieves. There must be some mistake.'

'That may be, but we have orders to search you and if you are guilty, then what do you think your punishment should be?'

The brothers thought they had no reason to be afraid; they knew they had not stolen anything, so they replied boldly, 'If the cup is found in any of the saddlebags then the one to whom the saddlebag belongs should be held as a slave to pay for the crime. This is the way we punish those who do wrong.'

So began the search of their baggage, and because this was a very serious and important affair, Joseph personally conducted the whole operation. To make the search look convincing every item of baggage was examined, leaving Benjamin's till the end. Eventually there was a cry of triumph and the cup was held aloft.

This was not a wicked plan on the part of Joseph to plant stolen property on an innocent man. On the contrary, it is here that we can see the beauty and intricacy of God's plan; though in Egypt, the law of Canaan in regards to thievery was established for this particular case of the missing silver cup. In this way, Joseph and Benjamin were to be reunited under the pretence of Benjamin having to remain in Egypt to pay for his 'crime' of stealing. This false accusation against Benjamin, therefore, was part of God's plan to bring Joseph and his family together again, to bring comfort to Jacob in his old age and to bring about forgiveness and reconciliation. Human beings may plot and plan, but God sees everything. In His universal plan human wisdom, like that of Joseph's, plays a role in undoing the evil plots of men to bring about good to all; what is apparently wicked actually achieves goodness in the long-term.

The brothers, of course, were unaware of this and were eager to distance themselves from this crime.

'We are not surprised that this cup has turned up in Benjamin's luggage. His other brother Joseph used to steal too!'

Instead of defending their innocent brother Benjamin, the evil in their hearts was exposed through their reference to a crime that Joseph never committed. If only they had known that it was Joseph himself standing before them and that their lies and treachery would soon be exposed!

Joseph, his face showing no emotion, thought to himself, *you have really made matters bad for yourselves now. Your crime is worse than stealing. God knows well that you are lying.*

The brothers were afraid of their father's anger. 'O exalted one,' they pleaded, 'He has a father, a very old man, who will grieve for him. Take one of us in his place. We know you are a compassionate man.'

Joseph, however, was adamant. 'God forbid that we should take anyone other than the person on whom we found our property. In that case we would be acting wrongfully.'

When they saw that he would not change his mind, they held a conference in private. The leader among them said, 'We all made a promise to our father in God's name that we would return with Benjamin. We have already once failed to keep our promise to look after Joseph; therefore, I will not leave this land until my father permits me or God commands me.'

The brothers listened attentively. The leader continued, 'Go back to your father and say that Benjamin has committed a theft without our knowledge. We could not have prevented something we knew nothing about.'

Could this be the same brother who suggested that Joseph should not be killed but be pushed into a well? Perhaps he was different from the others! His sense of honour prevented him from going back to face his father, before whom he had already been proven inept and guilty in failing to safeguard Joseph.

The nine remaining brothers returned home and broke the news to their father as they had been instructed to do. They asked him to check their story with the people of the city where they had lodged and the caravan with which they had returned, in case their father still did not believe them.

Jacob was completely devastated by the story. He knew Benjamin too well to believe that he had committed a theft. He could not, would not believe it.

'No, this is a story you have made up between you. But I must be patient. Maybe God will return all of them to me at the end, for He is full of wisdom and knowledge.'

Once again Jacob, as a man of God, did not reprimand his sons or kick them out of his life. He did not take his revenge on them. Instead, he submitted to the will of God and accepted His trial. He chose to be patient, maintaining his faith in God and in Benjamin's innocence, without complaining to anyone regarding his anguish and sorrow. Jacob hoped that one day his children would ward off evil, mend their lives and be good to avert God's wrath. He conducted himself in the same manner as he did when he was told that the wolf devoured Joseph. In fact, the shock of this new loss of Benjamin brought back all the old grief over the disappearance of Joseph. This double grief was such that his eyes became white with sorrow, the light of the outside world became dim and blurred as darkness covered everything. Jacob's grief had made him blind and, unable to share his sorrow, he fell into a deep and uncomplaining melancholy.

The brothers became exasperated; they had no respect for their father in his old age, nor did they have any sympathy for his grief.

'Will you never stop thinking about Joseph!' they exclaimed.

Almost to himself, Jacob murmured, 'I only complain of my distress and anguish to God, and I know from

God that which you do not know.' With this hope guiding him, Jacob sent his sons back to Egypt.

'My sons, go back, and enquire about Joseph and Benjamin. Never stop believing in God's soothing mercy. No one despairs of God's soothing mercy except those who have no faith.'

So the brothers set off once more for Egypt. When they arrived, they rushed to see Joseph; they must tell him of their father's pain and sorrow. They also wanted to plead with him to be charitable and give them more grain, even though they had brought almost nothing with them in exchange.

'O exalted one,' they said. 'Our father is suffering. He has lost his sight since Benjamin has been detained and, what is more, after all these years he has asked us to look for Benjamin's brother Joseph. We have brought very little to trade with, but we beg you to give us full measure as a gesture of charity; for God rewards the charitable.'

Joseph was moved to tears by the news of his father and he said, 'You know how unjustly you treated Joseph and his brother, not knowing fully what you were doing?'

The brothers were startled to hear this. How did this Egyptian minister know all this?

Then one of them looked closely at the man standing before them in all his finery and suddenly recognizing him, cried out, 'You are Joseph!'

'Yes, I am Joseph and this is my brother, Benjamin. We have suffered much but God has been gracious to us. He who is virtuous and patient is always rewarded by God.'

All that had been confusing for the ten brothers now became clear: the questions about the family in Canaan, the desire to see Benjamin and the inexplicable way that a silver cup had turned up in Benjamin's saddlebag. Surely the hand of God was to be seen behind all these events. Even Joseph's childhood dream was gradually becoming clear.

'Indeed God has preferred you above all of us,' the brothers said with realisation. 'And certainly we have been guilty of sin.'

Joseph was glad that they had at last seen how wrong they were and that they were truly sorry for what they had done, but he did not want to spoil this moment of reconciliation. Besides, he wanted to send a message quickly to his father, telling him that all was well. He could not bear to think of him blind and suffering alone in Canaan.

'Don't reproach yourselves,' he said to his brothers. 'God will forgive you everything and I too forgive you. Take my shirt to my father and put it on his face; then he will see again. Then come here together with all your families.'

Act VI: The Fulfilment of the Dream

Jacob, far away in Canaan, knew nothing of these developments. But even as the caravan left Egypt he sensed deep in his soul the presence of the living Joseph. When he told the people around him, they laughed at him thinking he was an old man whose mind was wandering.

Then, when the brothers returned to Canaan, a bearer of the good news from among them ran to cast the shirt over Jacob's face. The eyes which had grown dim with sadness could suddenly see again. Jacob was overjoyed; his faith had been rewarded.

'Did I not tell you that I know from God things that you do not know?' He said to his sons. They had not believed him when he had said this before, when everything seemed black, but now they came to see that he was right.

'O father, ask God to forgive us our sins,' they pleaded. 'For what we have done was very wrong.'

'I shall ask my Lord for forgiveness for you,' replied their father, 'For He is Oft-Forgiving and All-Merciful.'

The whole family, including Rachel's sister Leah, who had been like a mother to Joseph after the death of Rachel and was now married to his father Jacob, now set off for Egypt to be reunited with Joseph. When they came into the presence of Joseph, he drew his parents to him and said, 'Enter Egypt in peace and security, by God's will.'

He welcomed them all by entertaining them and providing them with homes. He treated his father Jacob and his stepmother Leah with special dignity, seating them as guests of honour on a raised platform-like throne.

They in turn, parents and brothers alike, bowed down before Joseph in recognition of his high rank in Egypt under the King.

When he saw this, Joseph exclaimed, 'Father, this is the fulfilment of my dream I had long ago, when the sun, the moon and eleven stars bowed down before me. God has made it come true. God has been good to me. He took me out of prison and brought you all out of the desert to be with me here. It was Satan who misled my brothers and set them against me. Now God has made everything good. My Lord is the most Gracious and Merciful in achieving what He wills. He is All Knowing, and Truly Wise.'

So Joseph, with a sound and pure heart, did not directly blame his brothers but instead blamed Satan for seducing and misleading them.

Joseph then prayed, 'O my Lord, it is You who have given me the power to interpret dreams and visions. Creator of the heavens and the earth, only You are the One I rely on in this world and the hereafter. May I remain faithful to You always and when You take my soul at death, take it as the soul of a man who submitted himself absolutely to Your Will, and unite me with all who are virtuous.'

That was the painful journey which Jacob had to travel to get the dream of his beloved son Joseph to be fulfilled and to save the rest of his children. It was his patience and faith in God's mercy that healed the wounds of jealousy and hatred that had been inflicted on this family. As parents, are we willing to go as far as Jacob, in order to save our own families in this life and the hereafter?

Act VII: The End?

The story is finished, but is it just a story? Behind the adventures of Joseph we can see the Hand of God, working irresistibly to bring about His plan. The good won through in the end, but not always as planned. How cruel of the brothers to leave Joseph in the well and to sell him as a slave! Yet Joseph became a great minister in a foreign land. How thoughtless it was of the steward to forget about Joseph in prison! Yet this left Joseph in peace until the time was ripe for him to come and save Egypt from famine. Sometimes it seems as if only wicked or thoughtless people have all the power and freedom in the world, but this is only our limited human view of events. God, Who sees all, will never let virtue go unrewarded.

The three roles played by Joseph's shirt in the story were amazing! False blood on the shirt to justify a crime committed by his brothers; a torn shirt to clear Joseph from false accusations by Zulaikha and a shirt with Joseph's scent to restore Jacob's sight. Of course it was not the same shirt. But we can refer to them collectively as 'The shirt of beautiful colours.'

Jacob and Joseph both embarked on two different rehabilitation programmes to save the other ten children from the wrath of God. Both father and son succeeded with the help of God, although they were not in direct contact with each other. It was their faith; the purity of their hearts and the true love they had for all members of their family that kept them going through the toughest challenges.

And the challenges were certainly tough! It is impossible to comprehend the extensive grief Jacob was put through; to lose your two sons at the hands of your ten, other sons would rip any heart apart. But Jacob provides a beautiful example of patience in this story. Despite the pain his children caused him, Jacob did not sever ties with them. He continued to communicate with his sons in the hope of helping them return to God's Right Path. It is this sincere and absolute trust in God that gave Jacob the strength and conviction to remain patient at times of loss.

Joseph, in order not to hurt the feelings of his brothers, claimed that Satan was to blame for sowing enmity between him and his brothers. Should we then blame Satan for our sins? Of course not. Satan says, 'Don't blame me, blame yourselves, I simply called you and you came running after me!'

Joseph was the victim and he forgave his brothers without any reproach. So whenever we fall into temptation and commit a sin due to our human weakness we must repent, ask for forgiveness and make an effort not to do it again. Our salvation is in sincere repentance. That is exactly what the brothers and Zulaikha did; they admitted their guilt and asked for forgiveness. They said, 'Sorry!'

Another lesson to be learned from this story is how a Muslim should integrate into a non-Muslim society without losing their religion or watering down their faith. Joseph fully integrated into Egyptian society; he mastered the Egyptian language, he accepted a high post in a non-Muslim government and he complied with the dress code of high-ranking dignitaries of the Egyptian court. However, Joseph never compromised his beliefs and continued to practice his faith throughout his time in Egypt; he never lost his identity.

We see in Joseph and Jacob examples of constant trust in God, during both the good times and the bad. Joseph also shows us the value of honesty, modesty and chastity. How easy it would have been for him to give in to the passion that Zulaikha had for him and to betray his master! How flattered he could have felt at the love of this noble princess! But Joseph's awareness of the presence of God and his knowledge of the difference between right and wrong not only saved him, but also influenced Zulaikha towards the path of true belief and selfless love.

Joseph could easily have forgotten his family once he became rich and well-established; but his thoughts always turned towards his old father and at the first opportunity, he brought the whole family together in prosperity. He could have rejected his brothers after all they had done to him, but he welcomed them and forgave them.

When death approached Jacob in his very old age, his twelve sons surrounded him with real tears running down their faces. He asked them a very important question.

'What will you worship after I have gone?'

They all replied, 'We shall worship your God and the God of your forefathers, Abraham, Ishmael, and Isaac, The One True God, and to Him we do submit.'

What an amazing father! Though the children were true believers, Jacob still wanted to make sure that he had fully discharged his responsibility before leaving this world, as a responsible father would. Jacob was not interested in distributing any material wealth; he was mainly concerned about the salvation of his children and their offspring in the hereafter. Such was his legacy! I wonder how many parents today are willing to follow the example of Jacob. He is, without a doubt, the greatest role model for any father.

Do not plan evil because God will foil your plan. Do not be jealous if you have less than what others have. Fight your ego to admit your guilt. Humble yourself before your Creator and immediately follow any evil you did with a good deed, it will purge it. Learn to forgive others, as Joseph and Jacob did, if you want God to forgive you.

Honesty, modesty, forgiveness, repentance, patience, selflessness, resisting evil, keeping family ties, being righteous and having trust in God; these are some of the many lessons we can take from the story of Joseph.

That is why it is called **'The Most Beautiful Story.'**

Chapter 2

The Sanctity of Divine Revelations

2:1 Introduction

This chapter focuses on three of the Scriptures revealed by God; the Torah (the Old Testament) to Moses; the Gospel (the New Testament) to Jesus and the Quran to Mohammed (may God's peace be upon all of them). In order to do this, the basic principles of the Islamic faith will first be outlined, followed by evidence from the Quran detailing how Islam is an Abrahamic faith.

In addition, two commentaries on the presence of Joseph in the Quran and the Bible have been provided. The first is by Abdullah Yusuf Ali (1872-1948), an Islamic scholar and former Dean of the Islamic College (Lahore) and is best known for translating and commenting on the Quran from Arabic to English. The second commentary is by John Kaltner, the Virginia Ballou McGehee Associate Professor of Religious Studies and Professor of Muslim-Christian Relations at Rhodes College (Memphis, Tennessee).[7]

Finally, selected verses from chapter five of the Quran (Surah Mai'dah, 'The Table', verses 44-48) have been provided to illustrate the sanctity of the Torah, the Gospel and the Quran and to show how these three Scriptures are revered in Islam.

---

[7] https://www.rhodes.edu/bio/kaltner (last accessed 24th July 2016)

2:2 What do Muslims Believe in?

In the Quran, God defines the Articles of Faith in verse 4:136: 'O you who believe! Believe in God and His messenger (Mohammed), and the Scripture which He has sent to His messenger (Mohammed) and the scripture which He sent to those before him (Mohammed). And who denies God, His angels, His Books, His messengers, and the day of judgement, has gone far, far astray.'

Islam means Peace and Absolute Submission to the One True God, the Creator of the heavens and the earth and everything hidden or seen. The only One to Whom worship is due. He has no equal - there is nothing like Him - He has no partner, and no wife. He does not beget, nor is He begotten. He is very close to us. He cares for us. We owe our existence to Him. He is Eternal, without beginning or end, Absolute, not limited by time or space or circumstances. He is the Most Gracious and the Most Merciful. He is the Lord of all the worlds. He is the Cherisher and Sustainer of all creatures and beings. He is the King of the Day of Judgement. He is the One Who accepts repentance, purges our sins and forgives us again and again.

The Quran shows that every messenger of God defined God to his people by enumerating the attributes of God. These attributes reflect God's mercy and compassion, as well as His anger and punishment. The messengers of God did this to distinguish God from the false idols of their people.

In addition to believing in the One True God, a Muslim must also believe in all Divine Revelations and messengers sent by God. Furthermore, a Muslim must also believe in God's angels, the Day of

Judgement and life after death. The following verses from the Quran will explain these articles of faith in more detail.

Verse 2:136 of the Quran reads: "Say (O Mohammed): 'We believe in God, and in what was revealed to us, in what was revealed to Abraham, to Ishmael, to Isaac and Jacob and the Tribes (of Israel), In what was revealed to Moses and Jesus, in what was revealed to the prophets by their Lord. We make no distinction between any of them, and to Him we surrender.'

Here we have the Creed of Islam: to believe in (1) the One Universal God, (2) the Message to us through Mohammed and the Signs (āyāt) as interpreted on the basis of personal responsibility, (3) the Message delivered by other Teachers in the past. These are mentioned in three groups: (1) Abraham, Ishmael, Isaac, Jacob and the Tribes (of Israel): of these Abraham has apparently a Book and the others followed his tradition: (2) Moses and Jesus, who each left a scripture; these scriptures are still extant though not in their pristine form, and (3) other scriptures, Prophets, or Messengers of God, not specifically mentioned in the Quran (11:78). We make no difference between any of these. Their Message (in essentials) was one, and that is the basis of Islam. [8]

God says in verse 2:285 of the Quran: 'The messenger (Mohammed) believes in what has been revealed to him from his Lord, as do the men of faith. Each one (of them) believes in God, His angels, His books, and His messengers. 'We make no distinction (they say) between one and another of His messengers.' And they say: 'We hear, and we obey: (We seek) Your

---

[8] Yusuf Ali, 1990, p56.

forgiveness, Our Lord, and to You is the end of all journeys.'

It is not for us to make any distinction between one and another of God's messengers; we must honour them all equally, though we know that God in His wisdom sent them with different kinds of mission and gave them different degrees of rank. [9]

In verses 3:84-85 of the Quran, God commands Mohammed to say: 'Say: We believe in God, and in what has been revealed to us and what was revealed to Abraham, Ishmael; Isaac and Jacob, and the Tribes (of Israel), and in (the Books) given to Moses, Jesus and the prophets, from their Lord: we make no distinction between one and another among them, and to God do we bow our will (in Islam). If anyone desires a religion other than Islam (submission to God), never will it be accepted of him; and in the hereafter he will be in the ranks of those who have lost (all spiritual good).

Therefore, anyone who testifies to all the aforementioned and submits and surrenders his will to the Will of God is known in Arabic as a 'Muslim' (one who submits). Submission can be defined as obeying God's commands by following what is lawful and avoiding what is prohibited, in order to achieve inner peace in this life, and salvation in the hereafter.

Verses 6: 161-163 of the Quran clarifies this submission even further: 'Say (O Mohammed) 'Verily, my Lord has guided me to a way that is straight- a religion of right- the path (trod) by Abraham the true in faith, and he (certainly) joined no gods with God.'

---

[9] Yusuf Ali, 1990, p120.

Say (Mohammed) 'Truly, my prayer and my service of sacrifice, my life and my death are (all) for God, the Cherisher of the Worlds; no partner has He: this am I (Mohammed) commanded, and I am the first of those who bow to His Will.'

2:3 Islam was the Religion of Abraham

Abraham is mentioned and honoured many times in the Quran and is viewed in Islam as a true example of one who believes in God alone. The Quran makes it clear that Mohammed is the last spiritual successor to Abraham and that both men (and all the prophets that were sent from the time of Abraham to Mohammed) were upon the same monotheistic path.

Verses 2:130-134 of the Quran affirm that Abraham was a monotheist:[10] 'Who can wilfully abandon the religion of Abraham unless it be one who makes a fool of himself? We chose Abraham in this world, and in the hereafter he shall be among the righteous.

Remember when his Lord said to him: 'Surrender!' and he said: 'I surrender to the Lord of the Worlds.' Abraham entrusted his children with this commandment, as did Jacob: 'My children, God has chosen the pure religion for you. Depart not from this life except as those who surrender.'

Or were you witnesses when death came to Jacob?

When he said to his sons: 'Whom will you worship when I am gone?'

They said: 'We shall worship your Lord, and the Lord of our fathers Abraham, Ishmael and Isaac: One God. To Him we surrender.'

That was a nation which passed away.

---

[10] Khalidi, 2009, p18-19.

They have earned their reward, and you have earned yours.

You will not be held responsible for what they did.

Verse 2: 135 of the Quran highlights the prophetic link between Mohammed and Abraham: They say, 'Become Jews or Christians, you will be guided (to salvation).' Say you (O Mohammed), 'Nay! (I would rather) the religion of Abraham, the true, and he joined no gods with God.'

The Quran, verses 3:64-68 clarifies Abraham's status as a Muslim (one who submits to God): 'Say (O Mohammed), 'O People of the Book! Come to common terms as between us and you: that we worship none but God; that we associate no partners with Him; that we erect not, from among ourselves, lords and patrons other than God.' If then they turn back, say you (O Mohammed), 'bear witness that we (at least) are Muslims (bowing to God's Will).'

You People of the Book! Why do you dispute about Abraham, when the Law and the Gospel were not revealed till after him? Have you no understanding? Ah! You are those who fell to disputing (even) in matters of which you had some knowledge! But why dispute in matters of which you have no knowledge? It is God Who knows, and you who know not! Abraham was not a Jew nor yet a Christian; but he was true in faith, and bowed his will to God's (which is Islam), and he joined no gods with God.'

Abraham's status is further exalted in Quran 4: 125: 'Who can be better in religion than one who submits his whole self to God, does good, and follows the way of Abraham the true in faith? For God did take Abraham for a friend.'

'Abraham is distinguished in Muslim theology with the title 'Friend of God.' This does not of course mean that he was anything more than a mortal. But his faith was pure and true, and his conduct was firm and righteous in all circumstances. He was the fountainhead of the present monotheistic tradition, the Patriarch of the prophetic line, and is revered alike by Jews, Christians and Muslims.'[11]

Verses 16:120-123 are also examples of how Abraham has been honoured in the Quran: 'Abraham was indeed a model. Devoutly obedient to God (and) true in faith; and he joined no gods with God. He showed his gratitude for the favours of God, Who chose him, and guided him to a straight way. And We (God) gave him good in this world, and he will be, in the hereafter, in the ranks of the righteous. So We (God) have taught you (Mohammed) the inspired (message), 'Follow the ways of Abraham the True in faith, and he joined no gods with God.'

---

[11] Yusuf Ali, 1990, p225.

2:4 Joseph in the Quran and the Old Testament

2:4:1 'Introduction to Joseph (Yusuf)', Chapter 12, the Quran', by Abdullah Yusuf Ali[12]

In subject-matter this chapter of the Holy Quran is entirely taken up with the story (recapitulated rather than told) of Joseph, the youngest but one of the twelve sons of the patriarch Jacob. The story is called the 'most beautiful of stories' for many reasons: (1) it is the most detailed of any in the Holy Quran; (2) it is full of human vicissitudes, and has therefore deservedly appealed to men and women of all classes; (3) it's eloquence consists in conveying many meanings for those who wish to learn wisdom by way of a mere word or hint; (4) it paints in vivid colours, with their spiritual implications, the most varied aspects of life-the patriarch's old age and the affection between him and his young best-beloved son, the elder brothers' jealousy of this relationship, their plot and their father's grief, the sale of the father's dearest son into slavery for a miserable price, carnal love contrasted with purity and chastity, false charges, prison, the interpretation of dreams, the swiftness with which ones fortunes can change, the ultimate honouring and exaltation of innocence, the sweet 'revenge' of Forgiveness and Benevolence, high matters of state and administration, humility in exaltation, filial love, and the beauty of Piety and Truth.

Not only is Joseph's story 'beautiful' from the perspective of its actual narrative, Joseph was himself

---

[12] Yusuf Ali, 1990, p544.

renowned for aesthetic beauty; the women of Egypt, called him a noble angel, and the beauty of his exterior form was a symbol of the beauty of his soul.

For the Parable all that is necessary to know about Joseph is that he was one of the Chosen Ones by God. For the story it is necessary to set down a few more details. His father was Jacob, also called Israel the son of Isaac, the younger son of Abraham, (the elder son having been Ismail, whose story is told in 2:124-129 & 37:99-111).

Abraham may be called the Father of the line of Semitic prophecy. Abraham was neither a Jew nor a Christian, as the Torah to Moses and the Gospel to Jesus were not revealed till after him. He was an upright man who had surrendered himself and his will to the will of God, which is Islam, (3:65-67).

Following the argument above, also neither Ismail nor Isaac, nor Jacob nor his twelve children were Jews or Christians. They were Muslims who submitted their wills to the will of God and never associated any partners with God in any form, (2:140).

God revealed to Mohammed, the final and last prophet of God, to follow the Religion of Abraham, the True in Faith, (16:123).

Jacob had four wives, three of whom bore him a total of ten sons. In his old age, his wife Rachel (Arabic name 'Rahil') – who was known to have been a very beautiful woman – bore him two sons Joseph and Benjamin (the youngest of the twelve). The place where Jacob and his family and his flocks were located was in Canaan, and is shown by tradition near modern Nablus (ancient Schechem), some thirty miles north of Jerusalem. The traditional site of the well where Joseph was thrown by his brothers is still shown in the neighbourhood.

The story is similar to but not identical with the Biblical story; but the atmosphere is wholly different. The Biblical story is like a folk tale in which morality has no place. Its tendency is to exalt the clever and financially-minded Jew against the Egyptian, and to explain certain ethnic and tribal peculiarities in later Jewish history. Joseph is shown as buying up all the cattle and the land of poor Egyptians for the State under the stress of famine conditions, and making the Israelites 'rulers' over Pharaoh's cattle. The story in the Quran, on the other hand, is less a narrative than a highly-spiritual sermon or allegory explaining the seeming contradictions in life, the enduring nature of virtue in a world full of flux and change, and the marvellous working of God's eternal purpose in His Plan as unfolded to us on the wide canvas of history. This aspect of the matter has been a favourite with Muslim exegetists.

2:4:2 'Joseph in the Qur'an' by John Kaltner[13]

The Bible and the Qur'an have a lot more in common than most people realize, including the story of Joseph—a soap opera-like tale of betrayal, adultery, sibling rivalry, and mistaken identity all rolled into one. Chapter 12 of the Qur'an is titled "Joseph," and it contains the Islamic account of the story of Joseph that appears in Gen 37-50. About a hundred verses long, the story takes up almost the entirety of the chapter; it is the longest single story in the Qur'an.

The Qur'an's version has the same characters as the Bible's, and the two texts share the same outline, with both describing Joseph's brothers abandoning him in a pit, his being taken to Egypt and thrown into prison before rising to a position of authority in Pharaoh's court, and his eventual reunion with his father Jacob and his brothers. As is typical of biblical traditions found in the Qur'an, the Islamic text has a briefer version of events, and it presents them in a way that supports Islamic belief and theology.

The most significant difference between the two accounts is the more active role God plays in the Qur'an as compared to Genesis. The deity is mentioned several times in the biblical account but does not have the level of involvement in the story that is found in the Qur'an. In moments of crisis, the characters in the Qur'an version rely upon God to come to their assistance. God reassures Joseph, after his brothers throw him into the pit, that he will survive the ordeal and confront them about what

---

[13] John Kaltner, "Joseph in the Qur'an", *Bible Odyssey,* last accessed 23rd July 2016,<http://www.bibleodyssey.org/en/people/related-articles/joseph-in-the-quran.aspx>

they have done. When he receives word of his son's presumed death, Jacob exhibits a level of faith and trust in God that is missing from his biblical counterpart. In the scene where his master's wife attempts to seduce him, Joseph does not succumb to the temptation because God is with him.

Once they are reunited with him, Joseph's brothers admit their guilt and ask forgiveness from God. God's higher profile in the Qur'an is due to Islam's view of the deity as the one who has supreme authority over all that exists. All of creation is dependent upon God and is subject to the divine will, and so God is intimately involved in all that happens in the story. Of course, this same idea is central to the biblical literature as well, but sometimes the Qur'an makes God's presence more obvious as seen here in the Joseph story. Another key element of Islamic theology is that God is not responsible for the evil actions of human beings. For this reason, the Qur'an mentions twice that Satan is the one behind the brothers' decision to rid themselves of Joseph.

Islam teaches that Joseph was a prophet, and certain aspects of his story in the Qur'an that are not in the Bible reflect this belief. The text repeatedly mentions that he has been given special knowledge by God that makes him wise and sets him apart from other people. While he is in prison Joseph delivers a mini-sermon to his fellow prisoners that instructs them on the nature of God and true faith, and he urges them to reject their polytheistic ways and embrace monotheism. His final words in the Qur'an are an appeal to God that he be allowed to die as one who has submitted his life to God (in Arabic, a *muslim*). The Bible and the Qur'an present a tale of two Josephs who aren't identical twins, but they certainly have a strong family resemblance.

2:5 The Torah and the Gospel in the Quran

There are many verses in the Quran which refer to the revelation of the Torah to Moses and the Gospel to Jesus. However, I have only chosen the following verses from Chapter 5 of the Quran to reflect on the guidance and light in these Revelations.

The Quran, verses 5:44-48 state, 'It was We (God) who revealed the law (Torah) to Moses; in it was guidance and light. By its standard have been judged the Jews, by the prophets who bowed (as in Islam) to God's will, by the rabbis and the doctors of law; for to them was entrusted the protection of God's Book, and they were witnesses to it; therefore fear not men, but fear Me (God), and sell not My signs for a miserable price. If any do fail to judge by (the light of) what God has revealed, they are (no better than) unbelievers. We (God) ordained in it for them: 'Life for life, eye for eye, tooth for tooth, and wounds equal for equal.' But if anyone remits the retaliation by way of charity, it is an act of atonement for himself. And if any fail to judge by what God has revealed, they are (no better than) wrongdoers. And in their footsteps, We (God) sent Jesus the son of Mary, confirming the law (Torah) that had come before him; We sent him the Gospel; in it was guidance and light, and confirmation of the law that had come before him: a guidance and an admonition to those who fear God. Let the People of the Gospel judge by what God has revealed in it. If any do fail to judge by (the light of) what God has revealed, they are (no better than) those who rebel. To you (Mohammed), We (God) sent the Scripture in truth, confirming the scripture that came before it, and guarding it in safety: so judge between them by what God has revealed, and follow not their vain desires, diverging from the truth that has come to you. To each among you We have prescribed a law and an open way. If God had so willed, He would have made you a single People, but (His plan is) to test you in what He has given you; so strive as in a race in all virtues. The goal of you all is to God; it is He that will show you the truth of the matters in which you dispute.

The Quran comes with a twofold purpose: (1) to confirm the true and original Message, and (2) to guard it, or act as a check to its interpretation. The Arabic word *Muhaimin* is very comprehensive in meaning. It means one who safeguards, watches over, stands witness, preserves and upholds. The Quran safeguards "the Book", for it has preserved within it the teachings of all the former Books. It watches over these Books in the sense that it will not let their true teachings to be lost. It supports and upholds these Books in the sense that it corroborates the Word of God which has remained intact in them. It stands a witness because it bears testimony to the Word of God contained in these Books and helps sort it out from the interpretations and commentaries of the people which were mixed with it: what is confirmed by the Quran is the Word of God and what is against it is that of the people.' [14]

---

[14] Yusuf Ali, 1990, p200.

Chapter 3

Joseph in Art and Drama

3:1 Introduction

This section focuses on the legacy of Joseph in art, drama and culture. Section 3:2 (Archaeological Evidence of Joseph in Egypt) highlights Ancient Egyptian artefacts that have been found, potentially proving Joseph's presence in Egypt. Section 3:3 (Joseph in Art, 13-19th centuries) looks at how Joseph has been captured in paintings and etchings around the world. Section 3:4 (Joseph in Literature and Culture, 17th-18th centuries) discusses the rise and fall of Joseph as a religious, moral and political figure in Europe. Finally, section 3:5 (Joseph in Film and Theatre) explores Joseph's cultural impact on theatre, film, television and animation in the 20th and 21st centuries.

3:2 Archaeological Evidence of Joseph in Egypt

<u>Middle East Media Research Institute (Memri) report on coins being found in Egypt bearing Joseph's effigy</u> [15]

- 500 coins were discovered in the Museum of Egypt in 2009; the coins were mistakenly labelled as "charms."

- One coin had an inscription and an image of a cow (symbolizing Pharaoh's dream of the seven fat cows, seven lean cows, seven green stalks of grain and seven dry stalks of grain).

- Joseph's name, written in hieroglyphics, appears twice on this coin: his original name, Joseph, and his Egyptian name, Saba Sabani, which was given to him by Pharaoh when he became treasurer. There is also an image of Joseph, who was part of the Egyptian administration at the time.

<u>Joseph is Imhotep</u>

- Belief that Joseph is Imhotep, a genius architect and administrator under the reign of 3rd dynasty king Djoser (ca. 2670 BC).

---

[15] http://www.memri.org/report/en/print3663.htm (last accessed 1st July 2016)

- Imhotep built a large complex in Saqqara Egypt that included the first ever pyramid (step-pyramid design, was to serve as future burial site for Djoser) and a system of huge grain storage bins. In these bins, grains and foodstuffs have been found.

- At the entrance of the complex, forty small cubicles were found; each just the right size to hold a single person who could administer the receipt of payment from people coming to purchase grain.

The Famine Stela[16]

Abstract:

The Famine Stela is an inscription that narrates a seven-year drought and famine that occurred during the reign of 3rd dynasty king Djoser. The stela is written in hieroglyphs and is located on the summit of the eastern hill on Sehei Island, near Aswan, Egypt.

Story of the Stela[17]

The story told on the stela is set in the 18th year of the reign of king Djoser. The text describes how the king is upset and worried, as the land of Egypt has been in the grip of a drought and famine for seven years, during which time the Nile has not flooded the farm lands. The text also describes how the Egyptian people are suffering as a result of the drought and

---

[16] Miriam Lichtheim, 2006.*Ancient Egyptian Literature: The Late Period*, p94-100
[17] Ibid.

that they are desperate and breaking the laws of the land. Djoser asks the priest staff under the supervision of high lector priest Imhotep for help. The king wants to know where Hapy (a river deity directly identified with the Nile) is born and which god resides at this place.

Imhotep decides to investigate the archives of the temple *Hut-Ibety* ("House of the nets"), located at Hermopolis and dedicated to the god Thoth. He informs the king that the flooding of the Nile is controlled by the god Khnum at Elephantine from a sacred spring located on the island, where the god resides. Imhotep travels immediately to the location which is called *Jebu*. In the temple of Khnum, called "Joy of Life", Imhotep purifies himself, prays to Khnum for help and offers "all good things" to him. Suddenly he falls asleep and in his dream Imhotep is greeted by the kindly looking Khnum. The god introduces himself to Imhotep by describing who and what he is and then describes his own divine powers. At the end of the dream Khnum promises to make the Nile flow again. Imhotep wakes up and writes down everything that took place in his dream. He then returns to Djoser to tell the king what has happened.

The king is pleased with the news and issues a decree in which he orders priests, scribes and workers to restore Khnum's temple and to once more make regular offerings to the god. In addition, Djoser issues a decree in which he grants the temple of Khnum at Elephantine the region between Aswan and Takompso with all its wealth, as well as a share of all the imports from Nubia.

Joseph's tomb and palace in Egypt [18]

- The remains of an older city (Avaris), which lies under Pirjaleses city, could prove Joseph's presence in Egypt.

- In Avaris, there is evidence of a Semitic presence within houses (bodies buried in sideways postures, weapons attached to tombs, objects in burial pits, Canaanite shapes combined with Egyptian shapes in architecture and home furnishings).

- These findings are consistent with Biblical claims that Semites settled in the Nile delta.

- David Rohl (Egyptologist and Historian): "A villa has been found in Avaris underneath a flat field of wheat. This villa is a small palace, however it did not belong to a king."

- The villa belonged to high ranking official and had 12 columns in the colonnade (a significant number in the Bible).

- At the back, south-side of the palace, a tomb topped with a pyramid was found. A tomb chapel was found in the tomb; therefore the tomb was clearly the tomb of a dignitary.

---

[18] https://www.youtube.com/watch?v=lm9ATLhkujY (last accessed 29th July 2016)

- In the chapel was a tomb statue that was vandalised. When reassembled, the statue was clearly not of an Egyptian dignitary: the statue had red hair and a distinctive haircut that was typical of Semitic people. The skin colour of statue was yellow, which was typical of how Egyptians would represent foreigners from the north. Red and black flakes of paint found on the robes of the statue, suggesting a multi-coloured coat.

- No bones were found in the tomb: consistent with exodus narrative in Bible which claims that when Moses left Egypt with the Israelites, he took the bones of Joseph with him.

3:3 Joseph in Art, 13th-19th Centuries

Below are examples of paintings and engravings depicting iconic scenes from the story of Joseph 13th-19th centuries.

Paintings

"Joseph's coat brought to Jacob", Giovanni Andrea d Ferrari, c.1640 (current location: El Paso Museum of Art, Texas).

"Joseph and Potiphar's Wife, Joseph leaving", Orazio Gentileschi, c1626-1630 (current location: Royal Collection, Windsor).

"Joseph and His Brethren welcomed by Pharoah", watercolour by James Tissot, c1900 (current location: The Jewish Museum, New York).

"Joseph interpreting the dreams of the baker and the cupbearer", Benjamin Cuyp, c.1630 (current location: Rijksmuseum, Amsterdam)

"Joseph gave orders to his servants to fill their sacks with wheat", illuminated Bible by Raphael de Mercatelli Ghent, late 15th C.

"Finding the silver cup", fresco in St. Sophia Church in Ohrid, Macedonia. C.1350.

Engravings

Print by Lucas van Leyden (1512 reverse copy engraving), which depicts Joseph interpreting the dreams in prison; Joseph sits in middle of print between two other figures, who are chained by their ankles to a large stone next to Joseph; above the head of each, a nimbus in which appears the content of their dreams.
http://www.britishmuseum.org/research/collection_online/collection_object_details.aspx?objectId=1337033&partId=1&searchText=story+of+Joseph&page=1

Print by Lucan van Leyden (1512-1550 (c.) reverse copy engraving) of Joseph interpreting the dreams in prison; Joseph sits in middle of print between two other figures, who are chained by their ankles to a large stone next to Joseph; above the head of each, a nimbus in which appears the content of their dreams.
http://www.britishmuseum.org/research/collection_online/collection_object_details.aspx?objectId=1336981&partId=1&searchText=story+of+Joseph&page=1

Print by Georg Pencz (1546 engraving). Plate 2; Joseph being lowered into the well by his brothers; from a series of four engravings. 1546 Engraving
http://www.britishmuseum.org/research/collection_online/collection_object_details.aspx?objectId=1453923&partId=1&people=51242&peoA=51242-1-7&page=1

Print by Raphael (1520-1540 engraving of Joseph recounting his dreams to his brothers, who sit around him as he stands under a palm tree.

http://www.britishmuseum.org/research/collection_online/collection_object_details.aspx?objectId=1470522&partId=1&people=51242&peoA=51242-1-7&page=1

Print by Raphael (1540 engraving) of Joseph revealing himself to his brothers who kneel before him in a hall with three cockle-shell niches.
http://www.britishmuseum.org/research/collection_online/collection_object_details.aspx?objectId=1470543&partId=1&people=51242&peoA=51242-1-7&page=1

Print by Anonymous (1540-1580 engraving) of Joseph telling the pharaoh of his dreams; roundel with the pharaoh enthroned at left, Joseph standing at right, courtiers in the background, a soldier in antique armour in left foreground.
http://www.britishmuseum.org/research/collection_online/collection_object_details.aspx?objectId=1494219&partId=1&people=51242&peoA=51242-1-7&page=1

Print by Georg Pencz (1546-1600 engraving) of Joseph lowered into the well by his brothers.
http://www.britishmuseum.org/research/collection_online/collection_object_details.aspx?objectId=1519338&partId=1&people=51242&peoA=51242-1-7&page=1

3:4 Joseph in Literature and Culture, 17th-18th Centuries

3:4:1 The Emergence of Joseph in Writing[19]

- During the 17th and 18th centuries the level of literacy within European societies increased considerably. Reading material had become more widely available and the 'novel' was recognised as the most prominent literary genre.

- In Joseph, people recognised their religious, moral and political ideals. Invited by the gaps left in the Biblical narrative, authors in the 17th and 18th centuries expanded, embellished, reshaped, dramatised and updated the Biblical story in order to highlight the relevance of Joseph as a cultural icon. An increasing acceptance of flexibility within the Joseph storyline permitted an introduction of innovative and modern ideas in Europe.

- The Bible became an "intertext": the parent or referent text of a literary work which is directly or subtly alluded to, and is recognised by readers familiar with it.

- Therefore an entire library centred on Joseph emerged over the 17th and 18th centuries, which included novels, stage plays, poems, children books and operas.

---

[19] Bernhard Lang, 2009, *Joseph in Egypt: A cultural icon from Grotius to Goethe*, p9-11

- The early modern figure of Joseph was not confined to literature; several of the textual sources listed in the following table mention paintings and illustrations, therefore adding a visual dimension:

    - In Grotius' drama, the brothers of Joseph discover and discuss a series of paintings in Joseph's residence that depict major biographical scenes

    - Zesen's novel includes etchings of Joseph

    - Goethe refers to a Joseph cycle painted by Frankfurt artists

- Artists and illustrators such as Remembrant, Murillo and Angelica Kauffmann have often depicted Joseph. The most iconic scenes that are most frequently depicted in art are Joseph being sold into slavery; Joseph being seduced by Pontiphar's wife and Joseph being imprisoned.

- The story of Joseph has also been expressed through music. Examples of operas and oratorios include:

    - Georg Friedrich Händel's *Joseph and his brethren* (1744).

    - Etienne-Nicolas Méhul's *Joseph en Egypte* (1807).

The following table is a selection of 12 works based on Joseph, written in Latin, German, French and English, belonging to a variety of literary genres, spanning a period of 177 years:

Author	Date	Title	Genre	Language
Grotius, Hugo	1635	Sophompaneas	Drama	Latin
Zesen, Phillip von	1670	Asseneat	Historical novel	German
Rowe, Elizabeth Singer	1736	History of Joseph	Epic poem	English
Morgan, Thomas	1737/40	The Moral Philosopher	Treatise	English
Fielding, Henry	1742	Joseph Andrews	Comic novel	English
Bodmer, Johann Jakob	1753	Joseph and Zulika	Epic poem	German
Voltaire	1764	Dictionnaire Philosophique	Essay	French

Voltaire	1776	La Bible enfin expliquée	Commentary	French
Lavater, Johann Kasper	1771	Christliches Handbüchlein	Children's Bible	German
Albrecht, J. Fr. Ernst	1792/94	Der keusche Joseph	Dramatised novel	German
Chateaubrind, Fr. R. De	1802	Génie du Christianishme	Treatise	French
Goethe, Joh Wolfang	1811/12	Dichtung und Warheit	Autobiography	German

3:4:2 Joseph in Teaching [20]

- Mothers and fathers told the story of Joseph to children at a young age in the 17th and 18th centuries. Educational theorists such as English philosopher John Locke and French bishop Fénelen gave instructions as to how to go about this task.

- Stages of imparting the story of Joseph to a child:
    - Tell the child the story.

---
[20] Ibid., p11-12

- Read the story: sometimes facilitated by children's Bibles that offered a simplified paraphrased version of the story, rather than the complete text. By the 18th century, really good children's Bibles were also illustrated.

- If a child attended a Jesuit school (as was the case with Voltaire), the child might witness, or partake in, a play about Joseph.

- Adults were also taught about Joseph:
    - In 1789, the French revolution gripped Europe. Lavatar gave 24 public lectures in Zurich on Joseph, in which he recommended the heads of households to assemble everyone, including servants, to tell them the Biblical story of Joseph (the educational role of parents extended to domestic help, who were viewed as child-like dependents on the family and were therefore entitled to receive Biblical instruction).
    - There are examples of the wider community within European societies being exposed to the story of Joseph. In February 1678, a protracted performance of a pious Joseph play entitled *Comoedie von Erzvater Joseph* (Joseph the Patriarch, a Drama) was staged in Dresden, when one of Europe's most elegant courts celebrated a family gathering of the House of Wettin. This social event, which was considered to be the culmination of courtly life in 17th century Germany, involved

pageants, banquets, hunting parties and the performance of a specially written trilogy on Joseph. According to a description of the event written later, the purpose of the play was to entertain the guests, exhort them to a virtuous and godly life and dissuade them from "beastly virtues" and vices.

3:4:3 Joseph in Literature[21]

- Three books that are discussed in this section: Zesen's *Asseneat*, Henry Fielding's *Joseph Andrews* and J. Fr. Ernst Albrecht's *Der keusche Joseph*.

- *Asseneat* is a German baroque novel that is largely forgotten today; *Joseph Andrews* is a classic of English literature which is still read today and *Der keusche Joseph* is a largely forgotten novel that portrays Joseph as a Hebrew freemason.

- Commonalities between these three works:

    - All three novels portray Joseph as a model of piety, endurance, forgiveness and chastity; thus the figure of Joseph expressed core Christian values and attitudes that were seen as unchanging and universally valid.

    - To highlight Joseph's virtue in the text, other characters appear in the narrative as essentially evil: the brothers and, more prominently, Pontiphar's wife who is seen as

---

[21] Ibid., p13-14.

one dominated and misguided by her passionate love.

- Some moralists believe that Joseph should not be brought up so explicitly in literature as an example of virtue, as moral writing can encourage immoral behaviour. For an example, German jurist Christian Thomasius (1688) believed that romance about virtue may serve as an aphrodisiac, promote libertinism and corrupt the reader because it opens the reader's minds to perverse imagery.

- Joseph was often represented as an iconic leader but not a traditional political figure in 17th and 18th century literature. This is particularly true in works that are focused on politics (e.g. Grotius' drama and novels by Zesen and Albrecht):

    - Joseph is portrayed as a rising member of the bourgeoisie and one singled out for political leadership

    - Joseph represented a new and improved version of statecraft: Grotius and Zesen in particular commend Joseph for his political prowess

- However a shift occurred post-1800; after the French revolution, the intellectual foundations of western society changed dramatically. The past no longer seemed to offer convincing examples or "icons" to rely on for solving moral, social and political problems. Intellectuals therefore became increasingly convinced that one could no longer learn from the past history. In this sense, Biblical heroes like Joseph lost their traditional authority in European society over the 18th century.

3:4:4 Joseph in Critical Thinking[22]

- Critical thought was applied to the story of Joseph in England and France in the 18th century, German critics later joined this trend in the 19th century.

- Three critics that are focused on in this section: Morgan, Voltaire and Chateaubrind

- Morgan believed the Biblical text veils evidence that Joseph was a power-hungry historical patriarch of the Israelite people.

- Voltaire saw Joseph as merely being a literary figure that echoed a Jewish tax collector working in the service of Egypt.

- On the moral message of the narrative, Morgan and Voltaire disagreed. Morgan deemed Joseph as a figure of despotism, whilst Voltaire recognised Joseph's generosity and clemency towards his brothers.

- When comparing Voltaire and Chateaubrind's critique on Joseph, similarities can be seen. As

---

[22] Ibid., p14-16.

practitioners of literary criticism, both agreed that Joseph was an eminently iconic figure (though one that belonged to literature, rather than political or moral life).

- Voltaire believed that the story of Joseph is an example of the oriental genius of storytelling. Chateaubrind, on the other hand, claimed that Joseph embodies the literary genius of the Bible, and therefore of Christianity.

3:4:5 Joseph: A Model of Virtue [23]

- The novel that is discussed in this section: *Joseph and Asenenth* (1st century BC-2nd century BC); a romantic novel about how Joseph, a paragon of Hebrew virtue, marries a foreign woman who worshipped idols but later rejects them in order to worship the "living God."

- Joseph is represented in this book as a model of virtue but in a stilted, limited capacity. He is introduced as:

    - Joseph the Powerful One of God.

    - Chief of the whole land of Egypt.

    - Self-controlled and virginal.

    - Worships God.

    - Meek, merciful and fearing of God.

- A strict religious observance on the part of Joseph can be seen in the text. In this novel, Joseph is morally pure, does not eat with non-Jews, acts properly around the opposite sex and refuses to sleep with a woman who is not his wife.

---

[23] D.S. Russell, 1987, *The Old Testament Pseudepigrapha: Patriarchs and prophets in Early Judaism.*

3:5 Joseph in Film and Theatre

3:5:1 Joseph and the Amazing Technicolor Dreamcoat (Stage Production)

Premise:

'Joseph and the Amazing Technicolor Dreamcoat was first performed at Colet Court in South West London nearly 30 years ago. Since then the musical's popularity has grown due to the countless school productions which have been staged. It is estimated that the show has been performed in nearly 20,000 schools and local theatres, involving 700,000 performers of all ages, and with an audience in excess of nine million. Today there are nearly 500 school and amateur productions each year in the UK.' (http://www.reallyuseful.com/news/joseph-benefits-bbc-children-in-need/)

'In September 1972 Frank Dunlop for the Young Vic directed the Decca album version of Joseph starring Gary Bond, at the Edinburgh Festival, where it was preceded by an act of medieval mystery plays that led to the story of the 'Coat of Many Colours'. In October the Edinburgh production played at the Young Vic for two weeks before transferring to the Roundhouse for a six week run. Michael White and Robert Stigwood subsequently presented the Edinburgh Joseph at the Albery Theatre, where it opened on 17th February 1973 and was accompanied by a piece called Jacob's Journey, written by Tim and Andrew with dialogue by Alan Simpson and Ray Galton. This told the story of the early life of Joseph's father, Jacob.

Unfortunately, it was decided that the combination of Jacob's Journey, which contained a lot of spoken dialogue, and Joseph, entirely sung, did not work and Jacob's Journey was gradually phased out. Joseph emerged to receive its first major production in its present form at the Haymarket Theatre, Leicester.'
(http://www.josephthemusical.com/uktour/about/)

Reviews:

Review by Ellen Ferrera (Short and Sweet Theatre critic for *the Daily Herald*): 'According to Ferrera, this [Joseph and the Technicolor Dreamcoat] production pulled it off with great energy and "outstanding" choreography. Ferrera was also impressed by the lighting and "minimalist" set design that was able to transport her to ancient Egypt. According to Ferrera, "it's kind of like a time warp.'
(http://www.dailyherald.com/article/20140325/entlife/140328873/)

Review by Diana Martinez (Theatre critic and host of the Short and Sweet Theatre review show, *Daily Herald*): 'The set, by Daniel Brodie, is a gorgeous backdrop for the electric concert-style light show, complete with powerful and artistic video projections. The musical director Wayne Green did a fantastic job of modernizing and stylizing a new sound for this classic score. The pop vocal riffs and updated arrangements give new life to these old favorites.'
(http://www.dailyherald.com/article/20140325/entlife/140328873/)

Review by Toby Zinman (Professor of English at the University of the Arts in Philadelphia, Pennsylvania,

USA, arts journalist and chief theatre critic for the Philadelphia *Inquirer*): 'In the course of much singing and dancing (what goofy choreography) and flashing lights, we've been taught lessons about envy, spite, generosity and forgiveness.' (http://www.philly.com/philly/blogs/363790991.html#FqeFPh6ZTpvc66vW.99)

Review by D.L Groover (Contributor to *Houston Press*): 'If you're feeling a bit sleepy when *Joseph and the Amazing Technicolor Dreamcoat* begins, don't worry, the show will slap you awake fast. And hard. This is the most frenetic show in memory, fast-paced, constantly on the go, terrifically cheesy.' (http://www.houstonpress.com/arts/joseph-and-the-amazing-technicolor-dreamcoat-slaps-you-awake-6371340)

Review by Mark Shenton: (associate editor of *The Stage* as well as joint lead critic): 'Superbly sung production that makes Andrew Lloyd Webber and Tim Rice's show feel as fresh as the day it was written.' (https://www.thestage.co.uk/reviews/2016/joseph-and-the-amazing-technicolor-dreamcoat-review-at-churchill-theatre-bromley-utterly-ravishing/)

3:5:2 Sold Into Egypt (Original Title: Giuseppe venduto dai fratelli- Joseph and His Brethren) 1961 Yugoslavian/Italian Film

Premise:

'A brother is cast out from his family, sold into slavery and then returns years later as a man of power - but shows forgiveness and compassion to his family through the strength of character given to him by God.'
(http://www.imdb.com/title/tt0056124/)

Review:

Review by David Johnson (DVD Verdict Judge for *www.dvdverdict.com*) : 'The story of Joseph is probably best known by its main prop, that snazzy coat he was wearing. But there's a lot more here, and the main theme, one of forgiveness, is as potent a moral as you'll find in the Good Book. **Joseph and His Brethren** tells the guy's story pretty well, and despite the obvious detriments it's got going against it—the age, the technical quality, some cheesy dubbing—all the major plot points are hit upon.' (http://www.dvdverdict.com/reviews/josephandbrethren.php)

3:5:3 Joseph in Egypt (1995 TV Film)

Premise:

'The Biblical story of Joseph, who was sold to slavery by his brothers who were jealous of his prophetic abilities to analyze dreams and of his being their father's favorite. Starring Ben Kingsly and Potiphar, Paul Mercurio as Joseph and Martin Landau as Jacob.' (http://www.imdb.com/title/tt0113483/)

Reviews:

Review by Peter T. Chattaway (previously regular film critic for *BC Christian News*): 'About as rich a three-hour epic as one could want from television: complex, challenging and convincing, it has enough emotional power to draw you into its world and enough realism to make you want to stay there.' (http://www.patheos.com/blogs/filmchat/1996/06/review-the-bible-collection-dir-various-1993-1995.html also http://www.rottentomatoes.com/m/1072918-joseph/)

3:5:4 Joseph King of Dreams (2000 Animated Film)

Premise:

'Based on the classic tale that has been revered through the ages, *Joseph: King of Dreams* is the thrilling account of a boy whose unique gifts lead him on an extraordinary journey. This inspiring all-new musical animated adventure brings the vibrant story to colorful life, showing us that we all have special gifts that can help us overcome obstacles. Brimming with action and drama, this universally loved story is still germane to today's families.

Joseph: King Of Dreams retells the story of how a boy's extraordinary gift of seeing the future in his dreams sparks a deep division in his family. The youngest of eleven brothers, Joseph is seen as his father's favorite. Jealous of this preferential treatment, the brothers sell Joseph to slave traders who take him against his will to the exotic world of ancient Egypt. Uprooted from his home, Joseph is suddenly thrown into a new life filled with high adventure, hidden intrigue and blossoming romance. After many trials and tribulations in this new land, Joseph is ultimately asked by the Pharaoh himself to interpret his troubling royal dreams. In doing so, Joseph saves Egypt from disaster and is rewarded with honor and status. As he rises to power, Joseph finds love and happiness. But a sudden twist of fate reunites him with his brothers, and the heroic young man must face a decision that has affected us all - the decision of forgiveness.' (http://www.dreamworks.com/homevideo/joseph/story.html)

Reviews:

Review by SDG: 'Artistically, the best thing about *Joseph: King of Dreams* is the visionary animation work in the dream sequences. It's here that this DreamWorks direct-to-DVD/VHS animated retelling of the story of the patriarch Joseph and his brothers comes closest to matching its astonishing big-screen predecessor, *The Prince of Egypt*.'
(http://decentfilms.com/reviews/josephkingofdreams)

'An Instant Classic Like *The Prince of Egypt* and *The Lion King*!'
Bruce Kluger, US Weekly
(http://www.dreamworks.com/homevideo/joseph/reviews.html)

'The Best Movie Premiering on Video This Year, and One of The Top Five of All Time!'
Scott Hettrick, Los Angeles Times Syndicate
(http://www.dreamworks.com/homevideo/joseph/reviews.html)

'Epic and Grand!'
Mike Trotman, Family Fun
(http://www.dreamworks.com/homevideo/joseph/reviews.html)

Awards:
(http://www.dreamworks.com/homevideo/joseph/awards.html)

- Parents' Choice Gold Award
- Film Advisory Board Award of Excellence

- Oppenheim Toy Portfolio Platinum Award for Best Video
- Kids First! Award for Quality Children's Media
- The Dove Award

3:5:5 Prophet Joseph (Yusuf the Honest/ Yousuf e Payambar) 2008 Iranian TV Series

Premise:

'*Prophet Joseph* is a 2008 Iranian television TV series directed by Farajollah Salahshoor, which tells the story of Prophet Joseph from the Quran and Islamic traditions. It is also set in the historical context of the Amarna period of ancient Egypt. They spend $2,000,000 for building cities and creating customs. Prophet Joseph is a Persian-language Iranian mini-series originally broadcast in 2008, which tells the story of Joseph according to the Islamic tradition.' (http://www.digplanet.com/wiki/Prophet_Joseph_%28TV_series%29)

Objections:

By Mustapha Suleiman

'Egypt's al-Azhar called for the banning of an Iranian series about Prophet Joseph on the grounds that it violates the prohibition of impersonating prophets in Islam.

The Center for Islamic Research (CIR), affiliated to al-Azhar, the world's leading institution of Sunni Islam, voiced their objection to the Iranian series Yusuf al-Sediqq (Joseph, the Honest) aired on Melody Drama on the Egyptian satellite Nile Sat.

The center renewed in its monthly meeting Thursday its concerns about the impersonation of prophets and expressed its reservations on the new Iranian series, said CIR Secretary General Sheikh Ali Abdul Baqi.'

(http://www.alarabiya.net/articles/2010/10/03/121082.html)

Bibliography

<u>Textual Sources:</u>

Abdel Haleem, M.A.S. 2005 [2004]. *The Qur'an, a new translation*. New York: Oxford University Press.

Ali, Abdullah Yusuf. 2010 [2004]. *The Meaning of The Holy Quran: Translation by Abdullah Yusuf Ali with a Brief Index.* Birmingham: I.D.C.I (Islamic Dawah Centre International).

Holy Qur-ān: English Translation of "The Meanings and Commentary". 1990. Revised and edited by The Presidency of Islamic Researches, IFTA [based on the translation by Abdullah Yusuf Ali]. Medina: The Custodian of The Two Holy Mosques King Fahd Complex For The Printing of The Holy *Qur*-ān.

Khalidi, Tarif. 2009. *The Qur'an*. Delhi: Penguin Classics.

Lang, Bernhard. 2009. *Joseph in Egypt: A cultural icon from Grotius to Goethe*. Cornwall: Yale University Press.

Lichtheim, Miriam. 2006. *Ancient Egyptian Literature: The Late Period*. Berkeley: University of California Press.

Russell, D.S. 1987. *The Old Testament Pseudepigrapha: Patriarchs and prophets in Early Judaism.* London: SCM Press Ltd.

Internet Sources

Nell Wyatt, Mary. "Joseph in Ancient Egyptian History." *Ark Discovery* (Last accessed 1st July 2016) <http://www.arkdiscovery.com/joseph.htm>

Kaltner, John. "Joseph in the Qur'an", *Bible Odyssey* (Last accessed 24th July 2016) <http://www.bibleodyssey.org/en/people/related-articles/joseph-in-the-quran.aspx>

29th June 2007, "Joseph benefits Children in Need", *The Really Useful Group* (last accessed 12th May 2016) <http://www.reallyuseful.com/news/joseph-benefits-bbc-children-in-need/)>

Suleiman, Mustapha. 3rd October 2010. "Azhar wants ban on Iranian Prophet Joseph show." *Al Arabiya* (Last accessed 17th May 2016) <http://www.alarabiya.net/articles/2010/10/03/121082.html>

Ferrera, Ellen and Martinez, Diana. 27th March 2014. "Short & Sweet critic Ellen Ferrera reviews Joseph and the Amazing Technicolor Dreamcoat, hosted by Diana Martinez." *Daily Herald* (last accessed 17th May 2016) <http://www.dailyherald.com/article/20140325/entlife/140328873/>

Zinman, Toby. 29th December 2015. "Review: Joseph and the Amazing Technicolor Dreamcoat" *Philly Stage* (last accessed 17th May 2016) <http://www.philly.com/philly/blogs/363790991.html#FqeFPh6ZTpvc66vW.99>

Shenton, Mark. 3rd March 2016. "Joseph and the Amazing Technicolor Dreamcoat review at Churchill Theatre, Bromley- 'utterly ravishing", *The Stage* (last accessed 17th May 2016) <https://www.thestage.co.uk/reviews/2016/joseph-and-the-amazing-technicolor-dreamcoat-review-at-churchill-theatre-bromley-utterly-ravishing/)>

Groover, D.L. March 19th 2015. "Joseph and the Amazing Technicolor Dreamcoat Slaps You Awake", *Houston Press* (last accessed 12th May 2016) <http://www.houstonpress.com/arts/joseph-and-the-amazing-technicolor-dreamcoat-slaps-you-awake-6371340>

(Last accessed 12th May 2016) <http://www.josephthemusical.com/uktour/about/>

(Last accessed 12th May 2016) <http://www.imdb.com/title/tt0113483/)>

(Last accessed 17th May 2016) <http://www.rottentomatoes.com/m/1072918-joseph/)>

(Last accessed 17th May 2016) <http://www.dreamworks.com/homevideo/joseph/story.html>

SDG, *Decent Films* (Last accessed 17th May 2016) <http://decentfilms.com/reviews/josephkingofdreams>

(Last accessed 17th May 2016) <http://www.dreamworks.com/homevideo/joseph/reviews.html>

(Last accessed 17th May 2016)
<http://www.dreamworks.com/homevideo/joseph/awards.html>

(Last accessed 12th May 2016)
<http://www.imdb.com/title/tt3084150/>

(Last accessed 12th May 2016)
<http://www.digplanet.com/wiki/Prophet_Joseph_%28TV_series%29>

(Last accessed 1st July 2016)
<https://www.youtube.com/watch?v=lm9ATLhkujY>

Chattaway, Peter T. June 30th 1996. "Review: The Bible Collection (dir. Various, 1993-1995)." *Patheos* (Last accessed 12th May 2016)
<http://www.patheos.com/blogs/filmchat/1996/06/review-the-bible-collection-dir-various-1993-1995.html>

24th September 2009. *MEMRI* (Last accessed 1st July 2016)
http://www.memri.org/report/en/print3663.htm

About the author

Dr Mohammed Essam El-Din Fahim was born in Egypt in January 1946. He obtained his Bachelor's degree in Aeronautical Engineering from Cairo University in 1967. He then worked in the aircraft industry as a member of an Egyptian-German team designing supersonic jets. Then in 1970 he left for London, England, to join International Computers Limited (ICL) as a Computer Programmer.

After obtaining his M.Sc. in Computer Science from London University he joined the R&D department of a consulting engineering firm. While working with them full time, he completed his Ph.D. from the London School of Economics, in 1978, in Airports Planning & Design using Computer Simulation Models.

Shortly thereafter, he started his own business as a project management consultant working on major construction projects in the Middle East. He extended his work in the UK to include businesses in the petrol, food and care of the elderly. He retired from the care industry in 2016 after 30 years of caring for the elderly.

Dr Fahim, in addition to his secular studies, has been studying Islam and its relation with the West since 1970. He studied Islam, Judaism, and Muslim Jewish Relations at Cambridge University and Islam and Muslim Chaplaincy at Markfield Institute, Loughborough University. He has appeared on and contributed to many programmes on the BBC and MBC radio.

He has delivered numerous talks to many organisations.

He is also an Executive member of the Three Faiths Form in East London.

He has organised many trips to the Holy Land for Muslims, Christians and Jews to show solidarity and deliver a message of Peace and Love.

In 1994 Dr Fahim was one of the Founding Trustees of the Qur'ani Murkuz Trust, which established the

South Woodford Muslim Community Centre and mosque. Since that time he has been the Head Imam of the mosque and the Chairman of the Trust.

His voluntary duties are too many to mention but include conducting marriages, family counseling and community chaplaincy. Dr Fahim is also the Muslim Chaplain to the Metropolitan Police in London.

Printed in Great Britain
by Amazon